PAINTING AT NORTHWESTERN: CONGER, PASCHKE, VALERIO

Notes

Painting at Northwestern: Conger, Paschke, Valerio is published to accompany an exhibition of the same title on view at the Mary and Leigh Block Gallery, January 24 through March 30, 1986.

Library of Congress Cataloging-in-Publication Data

Painting at Northwestern.

  Bibliography: p
  1. Painting, Modern – 20th century – United States – Exhibitions.
2. Conger, William – Exhibitions.   3. Paschke, Ed – Exhibitions.
4. Valerio, James – Exhibitions.   5. Northwestern University
(Evanston, Ill.) – Faculty – Exhibitions.   I. Mary and Leigh
Block Gallery.
N6512.P274   1986   759.173'1   86-775

ISBN 0-941680-04-5
ISBN 0-941680-03-7 (pbk.)

Painting at Northwestern has been organized by the Block Gallery with generous funding from Mary and David Green, the Alumni Fund of the College of Arts and Sciences, the Jerrold Loebl Fund for the Department of Art Theory and Practice, the Mary and Leigh Block Endowment Fund, the Hulda B. and Maurice L. Rothschild Foundation, and the Block Gallery Friends of Art.

Cover: left to right, William Conger, *Broadway*; James Valerio, *Still Life with Tomatoes*; and Ed Paschke, *Delamar* (details of Plates 12, 30, and 14).

Mary and Leigh Block Gallery
Northwestern University
Evanston, Illinois

PAINTING AT NORTHWESTERN: CONGER, PASCHKE, VALERIO

MARY AND LEIGH BLOCK GALLERY

NORTHWESTERN UNIVERSITY

Lenders to the Exhibition

The Alpert Family Trust

Robert H. Bergman

Steven Berkowitz

Lois and Bruce Berry

Roy Boyd Gallery, Chicago and Los Angeles

Barbara Caitung

Cole-Taylor Financial Group, Inc.

Mr. and Mrs. Jonas Dovydenas

Doris and Irwin Esko

Allan Frumkin Gallery, New York

Mr. and Mrs. Graham Gund

Mr. and Mrs. Kurt Gutfreund

Mrs. Ruth Horwich

Illinois Collection, State of Illinois Center

Illinois State Museum, Springfield

Phyllis Kind Gallery, Chicago and New York

Marina Bank

Dr. and Mrs. Larry Milner

Needham Harper Worldwide

The Northern Trust Company

William H. Plummer

Orrin and Joanne Scheff

Mr. and Mrs. Joseph D. Shein

Struve Gallery, Chicago

The University of Iowa Museum of Art

Catherine Upjohn

Private collections

Contents

Foreword

Painting at Northwestern: Conger, Paschke, Valerio is the first Block Gallery exhibition to focus on artists in the University's own Department of Art Theory and Practice. Since joining the faculty, William Conger, Ed Paschke, and James Valerio have brought a new excitement to the University as acknowledged master painters and as teachers. While they represent three distinct stylistic points of view, each has earned accolades nationwide for his achievements as a painter.

As faculty members, Conger, Paschke, and Valerio are building upon the fine art tradition established by past department members. This legacy has included, in recent years, Jack Burnham's significant contributions as both artist and theorist and George Cohen's influence on undergraduate and graduate painting students as well as his role in the development of Chicago-style painting. Conger, Paschke, and Valerio, along with others on the department faculty, are continuing this tradition of artistic excellence and innovation.

This exhibition serves as a mid-decade review for Conger, Paschke, and Valerio. Beginning with canvases executed at the end of the 1970s, the exhibition includes works produced during the first half of the 1980s. The selection of paintings, which was made in close consultation with the artists, represents their best works from these years. In that so many differences exist among the paintings of William Conger, Ed Paschke, and James Valerio, it is interesting that the time period highlighted here, and particularly the late 1970s, was so significant stylistically for each artist.

The exhibition catalogue serves as a compendium for each artist by incorporating up-to-date biographical and bibliographical information, along with writings by four guest authors. Dennis Adrian, also a member of the University's Department of Art Theory and Practice, has provided a thought-provoking introduction to the work of Conger, Paschke, and Valerio. Essays on the individual artists and the works included in the exhibition were contributed by Mary Mathews Gedo on William Conger, Michele Vishny on Ed Paschke, and John Arthur on James Valerio. Thanks are due these authors for their insightful and illuminating comments.

Much appreciation is due Rudolph H. Weingartner, dean of the University's College of Arts and Sciences, both for proposing the idea for this exhibition and for his support throughout its organization. The lenders to the exhibition also deserve our gratitude for sharing works from their collections with us and for enduring bare walls for a lengthy period of time.

Without contributions from a number of sources this catalogue would not be a reality. In particular, the support and encouragement of Mary and David Green are gratefully acknowledged. The ongoing support of the members of the Block Gallery Friends of Art and the Mary and Leigh Block Endowment Fund has also been crucial to the success of this project. Additional funding has been generously provided by the Alumni Fund of the College of Arts and Sciences, the Jerrold Loebl Fund for the Department of Art Theory and Practice, and the Hulda B. and Maurice L. Rothschild Foundation gift to the Block Gallery. Our heartfelt appreciation goes to all these donors.

Finally, it is to the artists — William Conger, Ed Paschke, and James Valerio — that the most lavish praise and sincere thanks must be given. It has been an honor and a pleasure to work with them; their cooperation, spirit, and talents are beyond compare.

Kathy Kelsey Foley
Director
Mary and Leigh Block Gallery
Northwestern University

Preface

The thirty canvases of this exhibition by William Conger, Ed Paschke, and James Valerio make a wonderful show for any lover of contemporary painting. Three sharply different styles are represented here, three distinct palettes, three deeply divergent conceptions of the relationship between canvas and the world. What Valerio, Paschke, and Conger have in common, however, is the talent, craftsmanship, and perseverance that convert impulse and imagination into finished work.

But the enjoyment that viewers of these paintings experience has an additional significance. Paschke, Conger, and Valerio are members of the faculty of Northwestern University. Each is a teacher of art who has a deserved reputation for being able to impart some of his knowledge and skills to students.

Perhaps the practice of art does not play a *large* part in a major research university such as ours. But by having Professors Conger, Valerio, and Paschke among our teachers, we signal that art is an *important* Northwestern activity. A goodly number of our undergraduate students are privileged to be able to study drawing, painting, and composition as part of their liberal education, under the guidance of teachers whose quality is evident in the works here represented. And each year, a few carefully selected graduate students have the opportunity to pursue advanced study of painting under the tutelage of these masters of the art.

This exhibition provides the opportunity to see the accomplished work of artists, each of whom explores in a stimulating way a different corner of the visual world. But we are also shown the work of teachers who, together, define for this time Northwestern's place in the world of painting. I hope that these canvases will engender pleasure on both of these levels, and that viewers will come to understand why we are so proud to have Professors Conger, Paschke, and Valerio on the Northwestern faculty.

Rudolph H. Weingartner
Dean
College of Arts and Sciences
Northwestern University

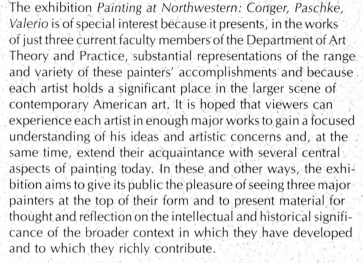

Painting at Northwestern

by Dennis Adrian

The exhibition *Painting at Northwestern: Conger, Paschke, Valerio* is of special interest because it presents, in the works of just three current faculty members of the Department of Art Theory and Practice, substantial representations of the range and variety of these painters' accomplishments and because each artist holds a significant place in the larger scene of contemporary American art. It is hoped that viewers can experience each artist in enough major works to gain a focused understanding of his ideas and artistic concerns and, at the same time, extend their acquaintance with several central aspects of painting today. In these and other ways, the exhibition aims to give its public the pleasure of seeing three major painters at the top of their form and to present material for thought and reflection on the intellectual and historical significance of the broader context in which they have developed and to which they richly contribute.

On the face of things, one might think it would be difficult to find three artists more separated in their stylistic points of view and artistic practices than William Conger, Ed Paschke, and James Valerio, and it is certainly true that the distinctive characteristics of style that each has evolved and developed are set out in this exhibition as strongly different. However, beneath this surface of separateness and differences there are some shared interests, which, manifested differently within the work of each artist, nonetheless allow them to be seen as a triad in which inner complements of concern may be understood and felt. After an abbreviated characterization of each artist's personal style, some of these commonalities will be touched upon here – not to suggest that the three men form any sort of hermetic grouping or share identical philosophies, but to point out some of the partly hidden correspondences among them that can enhance our appreciation of each.

William Conger's paintings have occasionally been described as one of the manifestations of *abstract illusionism* – a critical notion that fixes on the idea that while the artist deals in abstract forms that, overtly at least, have no representational function, these forms are presented with a conviction and sense of actuality that we associate with "real" things or virtual (i.e., representational) imagery and forms. While we may not be able to say *what* Conger's forms are (other than elements of his compositional structures), we do not question their existence within the mysterious spaces of the canvas (Figure 1). Therefore, while we can read Conger's rhythmically placed curved and jagged forms simply as painted shapes arranged on the surfaces of his paintings, we are more disposed, because of his subtle and engrossing effects of light and modeling, to see them as *within* the canvas, existing in a world at once different from our own and yet comprehensible in terms of it.

Figure 1. Detail of William Conger's Broadway *(Plate 12).*

Part of this effect seems due to the fact that Conger's shapes and the dispositions of them he shows us often suggest that they might perhaps be enlargements of the structures of such things in nature as crystalline rocks, microscopic plant forms, or some other aspect of the created world. At the same time, however, the scale of the shapes and the sweep of the movements of the compositions can suggest cosmic structures at the *macroscopic* end of the scale of created things. In this way, Conger's works have several kinds of links to our senses of perception of the natural world, even though they do not offer pictures of it; instead, the compositions seem governed by the principles and systems of organization (the *compositions*, in fact) that we sense are those of the natural world.

It is certainly true that Conger is a formalist, in that the compositions are the subjects of his works; in some cases, his content has the additional distinction of being addressed to the subject of the painting itself. This appears to be the case especially in those works in which the compositions offer quite a few rectilinear forms. These forms are usually set down so that they call attention to and interact with the scale and proportions of the rectangular field of the canvas. In some of these paintings, such as *Lakeview,* 1978 (Figure 2), the rectilinear elements not only refer to the format and especially the edges of the canvas itself, they also construct a windowlike aperture through which we see into a dark and enigmatic vast space, a "nightscape" that seems more the inner cosmic reach of the artist's vision than the reflection of some actual view. The "lake" in question is not so much an actual body of water as it is the emblem of the depths and vastnesses of creative imagination.

Figure 2. Detail of William Conger's Lakeview *(Plate 1).*

Conger's warm and vivid color adds a life and animation to his paintings that seem an additional link to the realm of actual experience. These colors establish an emotional climate. They also form visual organizations of their own that are a further dimension of the formal structure of the work and have a fascinating psychological effect of nostalgia, mystery, and enchantment in the way that they seem to glow with a light of their own, independent of any other source. This light is perhaps, again, a metaphor for artistic awareness and illumination, revealing to us things we could never apprehend by ordinary means. Certainly, this sense of the wonderful and prodigious in Conger's paintings is one of the elements central to their enduring interest and deeply satisfying quality as first-rate works of art.

Ed Paschke's painting has been seen as one of the most significant elements in the variety of artistic viewpoints called Chicago Imagism, since that critical term first gained currency more than a decade ago. Since his first regular exhibitions at the beginning of the 1970s, Paschke's painting has developed increasingly deep and complex aspects of both formal and imagistic issues. While many, perhaps, can see in his work only enlarged, highly colored images taken from the popular culture of club and show-lounge performers or film and television idols, such a view is both misleadingly superficial and inaccurate in identifying the artist's true focus. Paschke is a profoundly philosophical painter who, throughout the evolution of his increasingly complex style, has maintained a fascinating involvement with intricate questions about the nature of perception and our interpretation of it. His imagery, reflecting a repertoire of figurative icons of the print, film, and electronic media, poses questions about the nature of such images in relation to "ordinary" reality; how such relationships enter into the recognitive and identifying mechanisms of our interpretive processes; and (in the recent paintings especially) how such images retain powerul sets of meanings and trains of emotional affects even when they are radically transformed through the inventive compositional processes of the artist. If it is not too confusing to put it this way, Paschke's painting is about how we think we know about what we think we see.

These very serious and extremely intricate issues have to do with the larger questions of how we define ourselves in our visual and emotional environments, both "actual" and aesthetic. In dealing with these concerns, Paschke utilizes a rich and complex painting technique, identifiable at once by its very high, glowing color. His palette has an intensity usually associated with such processes as film or video, yet his work is obviously "hand painted" in a rather traditional way. In recent years Paschke has deliberately explored a whole range of paint-handling approaches, many of which may be found in a single picture. In such works the painting methods may range from thinly applied layers of translucent pigment that are seen as glowing washes to impastos that clearly sit on the surface of the canvas as individual weighty strokes. There is a certain paradox here, in that the artist's imagistic connections are with pictorial sources outside the range of the usual experience of painting, but the means with which he articulates his visions are more and more within the important tradition of grand-manner painting.

The monumental scale of Paschke's images, which gives them a commanding dominion over our attention, is similar to the commanding scale in Valerio's large canvases of outsize images. Within these large formats, Paschke makes, in his recent works especially, challenging demands on our visual and interpretive acuities, since the images frequently exhibit inventive "anomalies" that suggest electronic interference, slippage and division of the images, fragmentation and repetition of parts of the forms, and reversal of positive and negative tonal values (Figure 3). In order to rectify satisfactorily the faces and details of costume in the paintings, we are obliged to perform a sort of reconstitution of what we feel to be the "correct" form. That this process is itself analogous to the organizational systems utilized in the initial generation of the images is one of Paschke's main points, and his anatomization of our mechanisms of seeing and our systems of interpretation is among the most skillful of those of any living artist.

James Valerio's work, like Paschke's, is often superficially misconstrued as simply the pursuit of a painstaking (some would say relentless) interest in realistic vision. In fact, though, it is the result of a variety of complex steps, many of which actually *remove* the nature of his painted image from "real" vision. Valerio's paintings are usually constructs that involve the use of photographic projections and elaborate preparatory drawings, both as separate sheets and as part of the painting process, which make constant reference to related constructs both in photography and in other kinds of painting. If Valerio is a Realist, he is so somewhat in the manner of Chuck Close, who also employs projected and transcribed images originating in photographs the artist has taken. The sense of reality that Valerio's work projects, then, relates not only to how we see ordinarily, but also to how we see certain kinds of images (photographic, painted, or printed) that we conventionally regard as "realistic," even though it is clear that the sense of reality connected with them is a matter of their range and flexibility as *abstract visual languages* and not to any *inherently* realistic factor. Therefore, Valerio's paintings, while they present convincing images related to familiar kinds of artistic images (e.g. portraits, still lifes, models in the studio), at the same time emphasize the nature of these images as perceptual constructs that have their own rationale and structural logic.

Figure 3. Detail of Ed Paschke's Towanda (Plate 18).

This is perhaps what accounts for the hallucinatory clarity and frozen stillness of Valerio's work (Figure 4); these characteristics are the result of complex inner tensions, both compositional and perceptual, that the artist has very deliberately created. These tensions are frequently enhanced by Valerio's coloring, which, while often following what can be observed, nonetheless can have an acidic strangeness that seems arbitrary and even "unreal." These somewhat contradictory qualities are analogous to some of the internal dynamics that have been pointed out in both Conger's and Paschke's paintings, as well.

While the three artists have distinctly individual styles and have evolved them separately and with differing sets of concerns, the experience of the exhibition (if not these observations upon it) should reveal to the viewer some perhaps surprising areas of overlapping involvement.

Each of the painters is a painstaking and accomplished technician whose virtuosic manipulations of the materials themselves may be savored with the greatest satisfaction. This sort of expertise is always informative as well as rewarding. Although Paschke's handling ranges from thin veils of color to palpably substantial impastos, while Conger and Valerio present a more uniform surface, there is in the practice of each man a similar degree of concern for the unity of vision that the nature of the final surface can bring about. This unity, a focused sense of completeness and appropriateness, is essential to the force each artist wishes his paintings to project.

Also, each artist is interested in a highly rectified image and the presentation of individual forms, no matter how abstract, complex, or "distorted" the subject is or seems to be. The result is a sense of convincingness, of credibility, in fact, which ensures that we accept the visual world of the painter and can thereby experience most fully his formal, emotional, and metaphysical content. It will be noticed that each painter, while presenting a world of such conviction, at the same time displays a wonderful sense of invention and imagination. This sense of conviction that we feel is employed to give us the unique experiences each artist has created for us.

Through these kinds of experiences, complex and demanding as they may be on purely the visual or formal level, Conger, Paschke, and Valerio construct as well powerful emotional experiences that are apprehended in the realms of inner awareness and pure feeling. It is this level that the finest works of art must both structure and illuminate, for it is here that the most intense perceptions of what it is to be human occur. Our three painters amply fulfill this essential function of art and in doing so continue the highest standards of Northwestern's traditional commitments to the achievements and understanding of the humanities. ◊

Dennis Adrian is an art historian, curator, critic, and collector who has written extensively on Chicago art and artists. He currently teaches art history and art criticism at The School of The Art Institute of Chicago, Columbia College, and Northwestern University. An anthology of Adrian's critical writings, Sight Out of Mind: Essays and Criticism on Art, *was published by UMI Research Press in 1985.*

Figure 4. Detail of James Valerio's Pat Combing Her Hair *(Plate 28).*

William Conger

by Mary Mathews Gedo

It seems especially appropriate that William Conger should return to the campus of Northwestern University as professor and chair in the Department of Art Theory and Practice, for Conger spent the most memorable years of his early childhood in a home that his parents leased from the University, just a stone's throw from his present office in Kresge Centennial Hall.[1] The artist recalls the images and experiences of those Evanston years with eidetic vividness, especially the virtually daily pilgrimages he made to the shores of nearby Lake Michigan.

The lake continues to play a focal role in Conger's inner world as an adult, and his paintings and writings are suffused with poetic references to our mighty inland sea. For him the lake represents "a symbol of introspection, beauty, and feeling," a spiritual orientation for Chicago and its people. His paintings of the past decade reveal his growing preoccupation with lake and light effects, sensations he renders with increasing sensitivity in images that now sometimes hover on the edge of overt representation.

Lakeview, 1978 (Plate 1), the earliest Conger painting included in the exhibition, takes its title from the Chicago street that provides its fortunate residents with such varied vistas, an experience also alluded to in the central window-like image with its dominant ledge. In this painting, Conger set himself the task of portraying in a nonperspectival composition the relationship between a close, interiorlike foreground and a distant, exteriorlike background; the soft, amorphous sky views with their delicate glazings suggestive of fog wisps contrast with the architectonic window shapes of the foreground.

Lakeview illustrates one of Conger's two predominant abstract styles; since the early 1970s, he has frequently alternated between more rigorous, severe, and relatively static paintings like *Lakeview* and *Exile,* 1978 (Figure 1), and those in which more flowing, sensuous forms predominate, like *Electra II,* 1980 (Plate 3), with its botanical and biomorphic allusions and gentle but constant motion.

Conger's definitive abstract style developed during the late 1960s and early 1970s, after a period in which he had concentrated on representational painting, especially depictions of the human figure.[2] Unfortunately, the artist destroyed virtually all of these canvases; however, his occasional portrait drawings, such as the powerful self-image from 1983 (Figure 2), show the mastery of anatomy and draftsmanship that must have informed his figurative style. (His present abstract mode demonstrates a similar command of the principles of fine craftsmanship, for his immaculate surfaces and beautiful glazes reveal an unusual degree of fastidiousness and technical proficiency.)

Figure 1. Exile, 1978. Oil on linen, 52 × 48 inches. Collection of Mr. and Mrs. Lawrence Aronson.

Figure 2. Self-Portrait, 1983.
Pencil on paper, 18 × 17 inches.
Collection of Sarah Conger.

Conger's first nonrepresentational paintings all featured bright-colored, rather flat shapes floating on a light, often blond ground; it was not until he created *Flossy's Night*, 1972 (Figure 3), that the artist achieved all the elements of his mature abstract style. In this painting, he introduced a new background color, an almost black, red-brown hue; simultaneously, his preferred vocabulary of forms assumed a more evocative, organic character, revealing the allusive nature of his abstractions.[3] This new color scheme, with the dark, rich ground acting as a foil for the jewel-toned shapes, surface and ground alike veiled with delicate glazing, served as the prototype for most of the paintings included here. Many of the shapes he invented for *Flossy's Night,* such as the windowlike form in the upper center and the steplike configuration at the lower right, also appeared elaborated in the canvases that followed, such as *Lakeview* and *East Troy,* 1984 (Plate 9).[4] In fact, *East Troy* shares a direct thematic relationship with *Flossy's Night:* both pictures allude to the summer home that Conger's parents owned on Lake Beulah in East Troy, Wisconsin. But the landscape and water references of *East Troy* create a more cheerful impression than those of the darker, more melancholy *Lakeview* and *Flossy's Night.* In *East Troy,* the artist provides openings into his dark background, which lifts here and there to reveal the luscious, glowing light over land and lake. But, as if to underscore the personalized nature of this imagery, Conger has erected visual barriers to these vistas in the form of rather flat, ribbonlike bands (beautifully edged in light) that seem to prohibit us from entering the Troy of his private past, just as the debris of millenia impeded the archaeologists who sought to uncover Homeric Troy.

Figure 3. Flossy's Night, 1972.
Oil on canvas, 63 × 62 inches.
Collection of the artist.

Until he undertook the detailed study of our American past that inspired *Colonial Trespass*, the artist had preferred to imagine the colonists enjoying an idyllic existence in which they "just stood around looking at nature, as in Thomas Cole paintings." But his readings made him aware that it was "a time of rapid change, especially exploitation." The vigorous movement of these paintings conveys that spirit of change, while the zigzag shapes, especially those of *Salem Run*, express the more hostile, attacking aspects of colonial life.

The impressions of violent movement apparent in these twin canvases also dominate a number of Conger's paintings from the past five years that are based on Chicago themes. *Uptown Garden*, 1982 (Plate 4); *West Wind, Summer Sky*, 1982 (Plate 5); and *Red Night Chicago*, 1983 (Plate 7), all constitute painted commentaries on our urban atmosphere — the raw, violent, yet vibrant city scene that characterizes so much of Chicago and contrasts so dramatically with the tranquil impression its lake often conveys. In both *Uptown Garden*, and *Red Night Chicago*, the more static, angular shapes reminiscent of the city's skyscrapers serve as foils for the vigorous movement of the dominant leaf shapes. These sensations of frantic motion reach an acme in *Uptown Garden*, where the reddish bands in the foreground seemingly struggle to contain the choppy water, scurrying clouds, and wind-swept foliage the imagery so vigorously evokes.

Yet, as contemporary as these canvases appear, they also demonstrate Conger's continuing ties to the artistic past, especially the great tradition of Western landscape painting. Indeed, in both their painterly character and their violence, these pictures recall the canvases of such great 19th-century Romantic painters as Turner and Delacroix, two masters whom Conger greatly admires.[5]

But the canvas in Conger's oeuvre closest to Turner's many interpretations of the sublime and awesome elements in nature is probably *That August Day*, 1983 (Plate 8). The artist began this painting with the notion of making a formal composition with a large loop or curling element as the dominant shape. (*Lakeshore Chicago*, 1983 (Plate 6), presents a later elaboration of this same compositional idea.) This ambition proved difficult to realize, and Conger left the unfinished work behind to go on a vacation with his family.[6] He wrote in his journal of his trip through the Allegheny and Blue Ridge mountains:

The rugged contours of those mountains, the seemingly perpetual haze that hovers among them and, in the clearing of that haze, the stark contrasts between the dense green of the foliage and the open sky, together with the darkened and silent deep ravines with their continuously twisting roads, made a great impression on me.

With the mountains and memories still rising and falling in me, I came home to see the painting in a different light. That dominant — and restrictive — yellow loop curling in the center became a kind of prophetic summation of the mountain journey.... After our summer trip, these elements became the mountains, erupting from the earth 'mid night lightning, flame and smoke, with their precipitous ledges, spiky growths, and mist-filled skies.... [*That August Day*] is an expression of reality, a reflective and romantic acceptance of change, sudden and irrevokable, held for contemplation in the fiction of paint.

Figure 4. Salem Run, 1980. Oil on linen, 55 × 75 inches. Private collection.

Although many of Conger's paintings, like *East Troy*, allude to his own experiences and memories, others refer to broader historical topics. *Colonial Trespass*, 1979 (Plate 2), and its twin picture, *Salem Run*, 1980 (Figure 4), for example, grew out of Conger's interest in the history of America's early settlers. Although he is a notoriously slow painter, the artist completed *Colonial Trespass* in only two months — a very rapid pace by his standards. Once he had hit upon the notion of using the modulated light blue to deep violet background in place of his more typical near-black one, the space behind the foreground elements seemed to open up and the picture progressed rapidly. This was the first of his paintings to feature zigzag forms, and Conger liked the excited, aggressive feeling they evoked. He wanted everything in this composition to look fast moving, in contrast to earlier paintings like *Lakeview*, which seemed to him to be either static or quite slow moving.

If *That August Day* presents nature in a fearsome and awe-inspiring aspect, *Interior Season,* 1985 (Plate 11), depicts the landscape of the artist's mind in a similarly dark and threatening mood. Although the ostensible problem that Conger set for himself in this canvas involved the imposition of order and coherence on a painting composed of disparate elements, the bladelike sharpness and jagged edges of so many of these shapes suggest that the interior season to which the title refers must have been the winter of Conger's discontent. [7] The heavy layers of glazing covering the painting's entire surface underscore its intensity and *terribilità.*

What an emotional gulf separates the serene lyricism of *Late Day, Sky and Water,* 1984 (Plate 10) from the dark passions suggested by *Interior Season!* If the latter painting mirrors Conger's private demon, *Late Day, Sky and Water,* painted just 10 months earlier, commemorates a mood at once ebullient and tranquil, with luscious, curvilinear forms holding the more aggressive, invasive, jagged shapes in check. In this painting, as in *Last Troy,* Conger breaks his dark background space to expose brighter vistas of sky and water. The recurrent introduction of small, regular touches of glazing suggests the measured dance of tiny clouds across a light-filled sky, a progression mirrored in the echoing lake imagery.

The largest Conger canvas in the exhibition, *Broadway,* 1985 (Plate 12), is also the largest the artist has attempted to date. He painted it under a self-imposed deadline with the motive of adding a spectacular coda to his then-impending show at the Roy Boyd Gallery in Chicago (held in June 1985). Conger began the picture knowing full well that he would have to remove the canvas from its stretcher and roll it to get it down the narrow stairs leading from his second-floor studio. That meant he had to modify his usual working procedures. Typically, he begins with a tiny quick ink sketch that serves only as a general guide rather than a precise model for the composition. (Figure 5 shows the sketch from which *Lakeshore Chicago* evolved.) This procedure leads him to produce pentimenti-laden canvases reflective of the alterations in his design and color scheme as the work progresses. But the need to roll up the *Broadway* picture demanded a tighter, more methodical procedure to avoid producing a canvas with many layers of paint. Consequently, Conger worked out his preliminary sketch (Figure 6) in greater detail and larger size; he also included indications of value contrasts that he does not always add to such drawings. Moreover, he planned his entire color scheme in advance, rather than permitting it to evolve spontaneously, as he usually does. He began the actual painting campaign with another procedural modification: he brushed in the entire composition in values of brown before adding color; once he had achieved the subsequent color orchestration, *Broadway* quickly fell into place. Indeed, these limitations enhanced, rather than impeded, the artist's progress; he finished the canvas in exactly four weeks, a new speed record for this painter who has often labored four months or longer on much smaller pictures.

Figure 5. Sketch for Lakeshore Chicago, 1983. Ballpoint and pencil on buff paper, 2¼ × 2½ inches (image). Collection of the artist.

Figure 6. Sketch for Broadway, 1985. Ink on paper, 6 × 10 inches. Collection of the artist.

As he put the finishing touches on the painting, Conger began to realize that it was a special work in more respects than size alone: it summarized not only his work of the past two years, but a whole era in his artistic life. During those four weeks, Conger also received notice of his appointment at Northwestern, and the canvas assumed yet another layer of meaning; it now referred to the end of one phase of his teaching career and the initiation of a new epoch in his academic life, one replete with new responsibilities and possibilities.

The artist celebrated all these changes by creating a great visual poem to Chicago, for the picture's title refers not to the Manhattan theatrical district, but to the major Chicago thoroughfare near which Conger had lived as a youngster:

When I was a kid… I walked every day along Broadway. I was greatly impressed by the action and movement and noise of the street. It was earthy with its rushing people, shopkeepers yelling into the street, and newspaper vendors, the debris, the traffic, and of course, most dramatic of all, those wonderful clanging "red devil" streetcars. It was so exciting, so fleshy, so different from the serene and spiritual park and lake.

But Conger concluded his journal entry on a more somber philosophical plane:

My paintings show the danger, the fastness, the elegance and artificiality of the city. Also, they bring to mind the ever-present domination of nature and the transience of man's imprint on the world.

This reference to the finite nature of all man-made things reveals a meditative quality underlying Conger's art, one to which his journal frequently alludes. But if Conger, like many artists, believes that all art is really about death, he also paints like a man who fully intends that his canvases will outlive him. By crafting each of his compositions with consummate care, William Conger has created an enduring memorial, an opus that demonstrates once again the triumph of art over death — and of the artist over his own mortality. ◊

Mary Mathews Gedo, a former clinical psychologist, earned her PhD in art history from Northwestern University. Author of the book Picasso – Art As Autobiography *and numerous reviews and articles for art journals, she is also the editor of the journal* Psychological Perspectives on Art.

This essay is written in honor of my two dissertation advisers at Northwestern University, Professor Emeritus G. Haydn Huntley and the late James D. Breckenridge. It is based on interviews conducted with the artist over a long period and on notes from his personal journal; all quotations derive from the latter.

1. This building at 1818 Hinman now houses Northwestern's philosophy department.

2. Still earlier, Conger had painted in an abstract expressionist style. He believes that the beginning stages of his current canvases, with their freedom and deliberate roughness, refer back to that phase of his career. For many years, Conger has painted little panel pictures never included in any of his shows. He regards these paintings, with their highly experimental techniques, as a kind of postscript to his abstract expressionist era. Figure 7 illustrates one of these panel pictures from 1983.

3. As the current exhibition reveals, Conger continues to favor a dark background color much of the time. However, he never uses this background in a formulaic way, and close inspection will reveal that each "black" canvas included in the show varies from the others slightly in hue and value.

4. *East Troy* might best be described as a kind of hybrid painting that demonstrates both Conger's more geometric and his more organic modes. The artist deliberately set about creating such a synthesis in this instance.

5. Conger began keeping his own daily journal as a kind of homage to Delacroix and his famous journal.

6. Vacations have played a crucial role in Conger's artistic life. He frequently leaves an unfinished picture behind when he departs on a trip, then completes it in an innovative manner on his return.

7. Conger began this painting on December 30, 1984, as though it constituted a coda to the experiences of that year.

Figure 7. Lakeshore Arch, *1983.*
Oil on wood with carving and
collage, 12 ×24 inches. Collection
of Kathleen Conger.

William Conger was born in 1937
in Dixon, Illinois. In 1956 and 1957
he attended The School of The Art
Institute of Chicago, where he was
awarded first-year honors. He earned
his bachelor of fine arts degree from
the University of New Mexico in
1960. In 1966, he received his master
of fine arts degree from The University of Chicago, where in 1965 and
1966 he was awarded the Francis
Friedman Prize and a University
Fellowship.

Conger has received numerous
awards for painting, including the
Bartels Award in 1971 and the Cluse-
man Award in 1973, both from The
Art Institute of Chicago.

He began his teaching career in
1966 as assistant professor at Rock
Valley College, Rockford, Illinois,
where he remained until 1971. From
1971 to 1984 Conger was on the
faculty at DePaul University; he
served as chair of the art department
from 1971 to 1977 and 1980 to
1984. Conger has been a visiting
artist at Beloit College, The University of Chicago, The School of The
Art Institute of Chicago, and the
University of Illinois, Chicago. He
came to Northwestern University
as a visiting professor in 1984 and
joined the faculty in 1985 as professor and chair of the Department of
Art Theory and Practice.

One-Person Exhibitions

1965
George Williams College, Chicago.

1968
Alverno College, Milwaukee.*

1971
Burpee Art Museum/Rockford Art Museum (formerly Burpee Art Center and Museum), Rockford, Ill.*

1974
Douglas Kenyon Gallery, Chicago.

1975
Douglas Kenyon Gallery, Chicago. Recent Paintings.

1976
Krannert Art Museum, University of Illinois, Champaign.

1978
Zaks Gallery, Chicago.

1980
Zaks Gallery, Chicago.

1983
Zaks Gallery, Chicago.

1985
Roy Boyd Gallery, Chicago.

Selected Group Exhibitions

1963
The Art Institute of Chicago. Sixty-Sixth Annual Exhibition by Artists of Chicago and Vicinity.*

1971
The Art Institute of Chicago. Seventy-Third Annual Exhibition by Artists of Chicago and Vicinity.*

University of Illinois, Chicago. Five Chicago Artists.

Illinois Arts Council, Chicago. Illinois Painters II. State-wide tour through 1973 under the auspices of the Illinois Arts Council.*

1972
Joslyn Art Museum, Omaha. Twelfth Midwest Biennial.*

Theodore Lyman Wright Art Center, Beloit College, Wis. Fifteenth Annual Beloit and Vicinity Show.*

1973
The Art Institute of Chicago. Seventy-Fourth Annual Exhibition by Artists of Chicago and Vicinity.*

1974
The Bergman Gallery, The University of Chicago. The Chicago Style – Painting.*

1975
The Bergman Gallery, The University of Chicago. Eleven '75.

1976
Museum of Contemporary Art, Chicago. Abstract Art in Chicago.*

Krannnert Art Museum, University of Illinois, Champaign. Midwest Painters and Sculptors.*

The School of The Art Institute of Chicago. Visions – Painting and Sculpture: Distinguished Alumni 1945 to the Present.*

Crocker Art Museum (formerly E.B. Crocker Art Gallery), Sacramento. The Chicago Connection. Traveled through 1977 to Newport Harbor Art Museum, Newport Beach, Calif.; Phoenix Art Museum; Memphis Brooks Museum of Art; Memorial Art Gallery, University of Rochester, N.Y.*

1978
N.A.M.E. Gallery, Chicago. 6" × 9" Invitational.

Illinois State Museum, Springfield. Thirtieth Illinois Invitational.*

The Art Institute of Chicago. Works on Paper: Seventy-Seventh Annual Exhibition by Artists of Chicago and Vicinity.*

1979
Swen Parson Gallery, Northern Illinois University, DeKalb. Selections from the Permanent Collection.

1980
Chicago Cultural Center, ART/WORK.*

Mitchell Museum, Mt. Vernon, Ill. Chicago Artists.*

1981
The Art Institute of Chicago. Prints and Multiples: Seventy-Ninth Annual Exhibition by Artists of Chicago and Vicinity.*

1982
Ukrainian Institute of Modern Art, Chicago. Nine Abstract Artists.*

University Art Gallery, Sonoma State University, Calif. Chicago Abstract Painters. Traveled through 1983 to Eastern Washington State Historical Society, Cheney Cowles Memorial Museum, Spokane.*

1983
Arts Club of Chicago. Members Exhibition.*

Madison Art Center, Wis. Chicago – Some Other Traditions. Traveled through 1986 to Sheldon Memorial Art Gallery, University of Nebraska, Lincoln; MacKenzie Art Gallery, University of Regina, Saskatchewan, Canada; Sarah C. Blaffer Art Gallery, University of Houston; Loch Haven Art Center, Orlando; Anchorage Historical and Fine Arts Museum; Arkansas Arts Center, Little Rock.*

1984
Illinois Arts Council, Chicago. Abstract/Symbol/Image. State-wide tour through 1986 under the auspices of the Illinois Arts Council.*

Roy Boyd Gallery, Chicago. Abstract Painting in Chicago. Traveled through 1985 to Roy Boyd Gallery, Los Angeles; Lakeview Museum of Arts and Sciences, Peoria, Ill.

Arts Club of Chicago. Members Exhibition.*

The Art Institute of Chicago. Eightieth Annual Exhibition by Artists of Chicago and Vicinity.*

1985
Hyde Park Art Center, Chicago. Then and Now.

Arts Club of Chicago. Members Exhibition.*

The Art Institute of Chicago. Drawings: Eighty-First Annual Exhibition by Artists of Chicago and Vicinity.*

The Renaissance Society, The University of Chicago. Chicago White Sox Baseball Card Show.

*A catalogue or brochure accompanied the exhibition.

Selected Bibliography

Books and Catalogues

Chicago, The Bergman Gallery, The University of Chicago. *The Chicago Style – Painting*. 1974. Essay by Dennis Adrian.

Chicago, Illinois Arts Council. *Abstract/Symbol/Image*. 1984. Essay by Charlotte Moser.

_____ . *Illinois Painters II*. 1971. Essay by Whitney Halstead.

Chicago, Museum of Contemporary Art. *Abstract Art in Chicago*. 1976. Essays by S. Prokopoff and C.L. Morrison.

Chicago, The School of The Art Institute of Chicago. *Visions – Painting and Sculpture: Distinguished Alumni 1945 to the Present*. 1976. Essay by Dennis Adrian.

Chicago, Ukrainian Institute of Modern Art. *Nine Abstract Artists*. 1982. Essay by A. Morgan.

Lucie-Smith, Edward. *American Art Now*. New York: William Morrow and Company, Inc., 1985.

Madison, Wis., Madison Art Center. *Chicago – Some Other Traditions*. 1983. Essay by Dennis Adrian.

Sacramento, E.B. Crocker Art Gallery (now Crocker Art Museum). *The Chicago Connection*. 1976. Essay by Wilma Beaty Cox.

Articles and Reviews

Artner, Alan. "Art: William Conger." *Chicago Tribune* (April 21, 1978): 3/10.

_____ . "Art: William Conger." *Chicago Tribune* (May 16, 1980): 3/11.

_____ . "Art: William Conger." *Chicago Tribune* (February 25, 1983): 3/16.

_____ . "Conger Exhibit Offers a Richness of Color." *Chicago Tribune* (July 5, 1985): 7/45-46.

_____ . "From DeKooning to Kitsch, Five Causes for Local Celebration." *Chicago Tribune* (December 21, 1975): 6/7.

Bonesteel, Michael. "William Conger." *Art in America* 73 (November 1985): 169-70.

Campbell, Lawrence. "Reviews and Previews: New Names this Month." *Art News* 58 (February 1960): 18.

Conger, William. "Letters: Attitude Toward Form Unites Chicago Painting." *New Art Examiner* 9 (June 1982): 2.

Gedo, Mary Mathews. "Abstraction as Metaphor: The Evocative Imagery of William Conger, Miyoko Ito, Richard Loving and Frank Piatek." *Arts Magazine* 57 (October 1982): 112-17.

_____ . "Interconnections: A Study of Chicago Style Relationships in Painting." *Arts Magazine* 58 (September 1983): 92-97.

_____ . "Reviews: William Conger." *Arts Magazine* 57 (June 1983): 47.

_____ . "Speakeasy." *New Art Examiner* 12 (April 1985): 12-14.

Guthrie, Derek. "Reviews: William Conger." *New Art Examiner* 3 (February 1976): 13.

Haydon, Harold. "Art: Colors and Hues." *Chicago Sun-Times* (January 20, 1974): 3/10.

_____ . "Art: William Conger." *Chicago Sun-Times* (May 23, 1980): 3/3.

_____ . "Art: William Conger." *Chicago Sun-Times* (March 11, 1983): 2/30.

_____ . "A Wealth of Abstract Art in Chicago." *Chicago Sun-Times* (February 29, 1976): 4/1, 8.

Henry, Alan. "Auctions: Fund-Raiser Teams Baseball, Art." *Chicago Sun-Times* (June 28, 1985): 84.

Lyon, Christopher. "Abstract Mode Well-Represented." *Chicago Sun-Times* (October 5, 1984): Guide/3.

_____ . "Coming in from the Cold." *Chicago* (May 1984): 156-69; 196, 198.

_____ . "The Nation: Abstract/Symbol/Image." *Art News* 83 (December 1984): 131-34.

Morgan, A. "Chicago Artists." *New Art Examiner* 11 (Summer 1983): 18.

Morrison, C.L. "Reviews: Bill Conger." *Artforum* 14 (March 1976): 74.

_____ . "Reviews: Bill Conger." *Artforum* 16 (Summer 1978): 79.

_____ . "Reviews: The Chicago Connection." *Artforum* 15 (February 1977): 73.

Moser, Charlotte. "Regional Revisions: Houston and Chicago." *Art in America* 73 (July 1985): 90-99.

_____ . "William Conger." *Art News* 84 (September 1985): 119-20.

Schulze, Franz. "Art: William Conger." *Chicago Sun-Times* (April 7, 1978): 76.

_____ . "Chicago: Bigger and Livelier But..." *Art News* 78 (February 1979): 40-45.

_____ . "Chicago, Nothing But Abstract." *Art News* 75 (Summer 1976): 154-57.

Taylor, Sue. "Reviews: Abstract/Symbol/Image." *New Art Examiner* 12 (December 1984): 61-62.

Yood, James. "Reviews: William Conger." *New Art Examiner* 13 (October 1985): 57.

William Conger

1

Lakeview 1978
Oil on canvas
60 × 54 inches
Collection of the Illinois State
Museum, Springfield

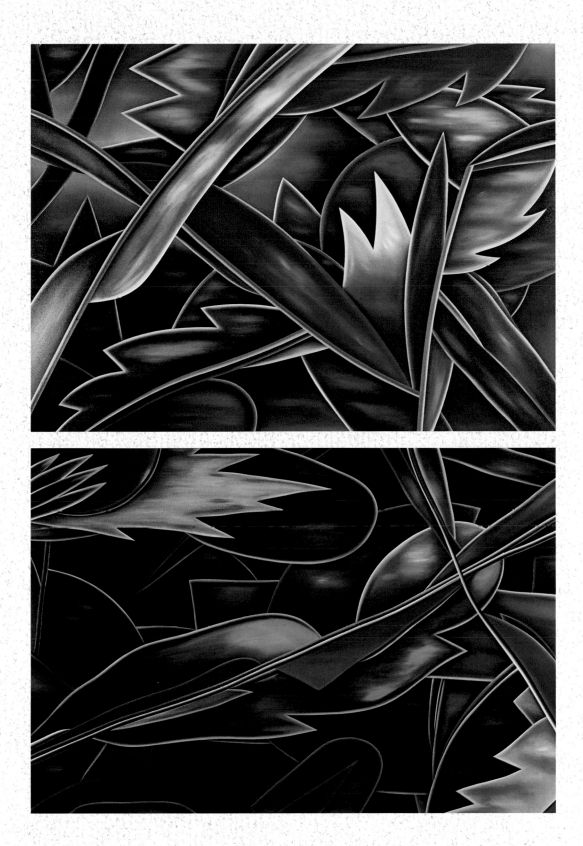

2
Colonial Trespass 1979
Oil on canvas
55 × 75 inches
Collection of
Mr. and Mrs. Jonas Dovydenas

3
Electra II 1980
Oil on linen
57 × 84 inches
Collection of Needham Harper
Worldwide

4

Uptown Garden 1982
Oil on linen
54 × 72 inches
Collection of Catherine Upjohn

5

West Wind, Summer Sky 1982
Oil on linen
54×72 inches
Collection of Marina Bank

6

Lakeshore Chicago 1983
Oil on linen
60 × 70 inches
Collection of
Mr. and Mrs. Kurt Gutfreund

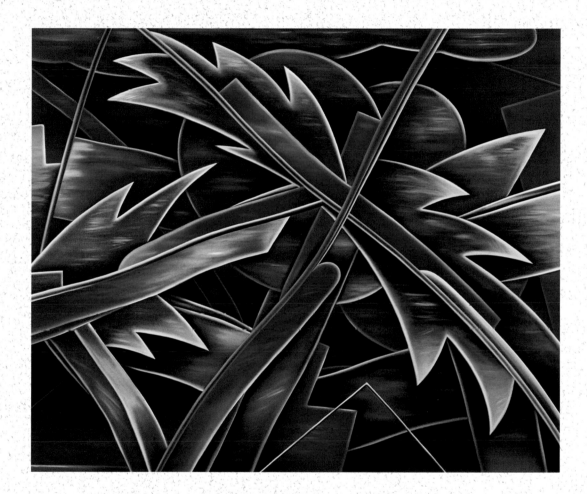

7

Red Night Chicago 1983
Oil on canvas
60 × 72 inches
Collection of Cole-Taylor
Financial Group, Inc.

8

That August Day 1983
Oil on linen
60 × 72 inches
Collection of Barbara Caitung

10

Late Day, Sky and Water 1984
Oil on linen
44 × 40 inches
Private collection

9

East Troy 1984
Oil on linen
48 × 40 inches
Private collection

11

Interior Season 1985
Oil on linen
48 × 44 inches
Collection of Mrs. Ruth Horwich

12

Broadway 1985
Oil on canvas
68 × 120 inches
Courtesy of Roy Boyd Gallery,
Chicago and Los Angeles

Ed Paschke

by Michele Vishny

Figure 1. Nervosa, 1980.
Oil on canvas, 46×42 inches.
Collection of Judith and
Edward Neisser.

The French art historian and critic Henri Focillon stated that "although each individual is contemporary first of all with himself and with his generation, he is also contemporary with the spiritual group of which he is a member."[1] Ed Paschke's spiritual group consists of artists who choose to portray the human condition. Among the hundreds of paintings he has created over the past 20 years, one example suffices: *Nervosa,* 1980 (Figure 1). In its expression of brooding depression, it has affinities with such works as *Melencolia I* by Dürer, *Jeremiah* by Michelangelo, *The Thinker* by Rodin, and *Evening/Melancholy* by Munch. All of these artists depicted the body and its various postures and movements to convey emotional states. Paschke works within this tradition but imposes stricter limits on himself by concentrating on heads, torsos, and a few hand gestures. Although they portray the most mundane attitudes and reflect repeated investigations of similar motifs, the paintings are richly varied and intensely powerful.

Paschke's art is frequently characterized as *confrontational.* This term not only seems relevant to today's work, but also correctly describes reactions to his pictures since the mid-1960s. Though related to Pop Art, Paschke's early paintings do not portray its glorified icons but, instead, cheap amusements such as circus freak and burlesque shows, boxing and wrestling matches, and porno films. What polite society rejected was grist for Paschke's mill. While Warhol pleased with glamorous images of Marilyn and Jackie, Paschke provoked with paintings of a freak show fat woman and Lee Harvey Oswald (for example, *Heavy Lady* and *Purple Ritual,* both 1967).[2] The disparate imagery in the pictures of this period suggest collage. They depict politicians, baseball stars, strippers, and cowboys, together with English, Spanish, or Chinese lettering and American patriotic emblems. Though reds and yellows abound, most of the paintings are rather dark because of the black grounds favored by Paschke as a means of overcoming a fear of making the first marks and perhaps spoiling the white, empty canvas.[3]

In 1969 several changes occurred, all of which appeared in *Ramrod* (Figure 2): the scale of the figures increased, with pictures sometimes concentrating on one person; the imagery became more shocking, assaulting the viewer's sensibilities with its combination of blatant male and female sexuality in one character; and finally, the masked face appeared, an iconographic element that is very much a part of Paschke's work today, though it has undergone radical formal changes. *Ramrod* examines role playing in its presentation of opposites, among them, male and female, face and mask, and man and mouse. It is a subject that Paschke continues to explore in his painting.

If the he-man was the favorite vehicle for presenting role playing in 1969 (some other examples are *Mid American, Muscle Man, Sunburn*), the accordion-playing entertainer supplanted him as the subject of more than half of Paschke's production the following year. With a vengeance he foisted this instrument onto unknowns and celebrities alike (for example, Marilyn Monroe and Frank Sinatra, Figure 3). By showing them with this mundane instrument, he deflated the stardom of the celebrities, thereby raising some probing questions about the powerful associations we attach to inanimate objects.

Figure 3. Tiger Rag, *1970.*
Oil on canvas, 63 × 50 inches.
Collection of Mr. and Mrs.
Jerome H. Torshen.

Figure 2. Ramrod, *1969. Oil*
on canvas, 44 × 25¾ inches.
Jones/Faulkner Collection.

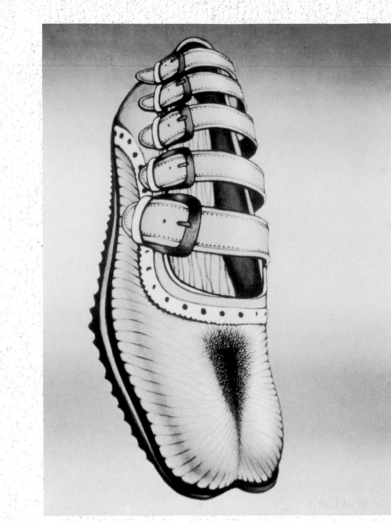

Figure 4. Yellow Wave, 1972.
Oil on canvas, 32 × 24 inches.
Collection of Stefan T. Edlis.

Figure 5. Elcina, 1973. Oil
on canvas, 60 × 38¼ inches.
Collection of the Museum of
Contemporary Art, gift of
Mr. Albert J. Bildner.

Figure 6. Quinten Massys, A
Grotesque Old Woman ("The Ugly
Duchess") ca. 1525, Reproduced
by courtesy of the Trustees,
The National Gallery, London.

Other paintings of this early period feature small images of shoes and gloves, which, along with leather handbags, were to become the sole subjects of most of Paschke's work from 1971 to 1973. While fantasizing on the objects' earlier state, when the animal hide was living tissue, he also viewed them as reflections of the human condition, as in *Yellow Wave*, 1972 (Figure 4). Embellished with hair, warts, and other growths, together with distortions of shape to suggest sexual organs, the objects display human characteristics. To the artist, these anthropomorphic creations are somehow counterparts of people with tattooed flesh (also a frequent early subject) who treat their skin as though it were leather to be tooled.

This concentration on the inanimate stimulated Paschke's imagination even further, so that when he returned to rendering the human figure, there were extravagant new inventions. Paschke concocted some of the most bizarre details of costume ever created for his garish cast of characters, who also sport coiffures that perhaps caricature the bouffant hairdos that were once stylish. First he painted a series of women (mainly showgirls and strippers), many with hornlike hairdos somewhat reminiscent of Quinten Massys' so-called *"Ugly Duchess,"* itself a satirical exaggeration of 15th-century Flemish hairstyles (Figures 5 and 6).

These wild women, products of an unbounded imagination, earned Paschke an undeserved reputation as a misogynist. This was dispelled by his ensuing portrayals of men, peacocks such as *Jesus* of 1974 or *Armondo* of 1975 flaunting equally absurd clothing and hairstyles (Figure 7). Paschke's technical bravura in handling textures is here displayed to its utmost in the rich patterning of the costumes and the luxuriant satin-surfaced backgrounds (the latter evolving from a series of abstract canvases of patterned color fields that were concurrently produced).

In 1977 Paschke's work took new directions. No longer interested in rendering the three-dimensional aspects of his subjects, he made the human head illusive. It existed, for example, as a piece of drapery behind massive sunglasses or a ghostlike sheet so tubular that it suggested a cylinder beneath. In a few pictures, he eliminated the head altogether.[4] Another change was the introduction of wavelike neon lines, first evident in two small mask paintings, *Signaturo* and *Signatura*, which derived their titles from Paschke's electrolinear signature behind the eyeholes. These lines, together with spectral bands of color that evolved a few years later, suggest malfunctioning television. For centuries, artists' canvases were treated as windows allowing the viewer to look in on the person portrayed. Paschke's canvas, however, is more analogous to a video screen flashing two-dimensional figures that are more shadow than substance. Whereas Renaissance portraits were individualized renderings of people and their environment, Paschke's anonymous individuals, with their prosaic gestures – hands adjusting hats or eyeglasses or stifling a yawn – perhaps convey the superficiality of modern life. Although these pictures frequently appear to be executed with an airbrush, all of Paschke's work is created by traditional methods. A careful building up of layers of transparent and opaque colors even produces his more recent images resembling X-rays or photographic negatives.

Radio-TV (Plate 13), the earliest work included here, bears the dates 1977 and 1980. Essentially completed in 1977, it was exhibited in Paris the following year with a number of other works depicting formally clothed entertainers. The canvas was then called *Ontiveros*, named for Steve Ontiveros, a Chicago Cubs baseball player.[5] (As with most of Paschke's paintings, the title has nothing to do with the content of the work, but conveys a sound or flavor he finds appealing.) The particularly strong impact the painting made may have been due in part to its sheer size, one of his largest canvases to date. Another factor, of course, is its imagery, for example, the headless torsos in tuxedos, neither human beings nor mannequins, which seem to have materialized from some mysterious realm.

As noted above, strange substitutes for the head were made in several 1977 works, such as *Cha-Cho*, in which a ruffled shirt extends upward ad infinitum on a figure whose pose is identical to those in the background of *Radio-TV*. When questioned about these somewhat gruesome images, Paschke explained that he "grew tired of the literalness in the faces" of his prior works. When *Ontiveros* underwent minor modifications in 1980, childrens' drawings were a source for its imagery. Crudely drawn television sets were added across the red dinner jacket in the foreground in order to break up this large, relatively smooth area and to serve as a contrast to its formality. These changes suggested the new title, but *Radio-TV* neither describes nor elucidates this hypnotic work.

Figure 7. Armondo, 1975. Oil on canvas, 84 ×48 inches. Collection of Mr. and Mrs. Lawrence Aronson.

With the exception of one painting, *Meyamo,* to be discussed below, the remainder of the canvases in this exhibition present two or more figures linked together by bands of color or merging forms. But what their interrelationships signify and what is taking place cannot easily be stated. This is what Paschke intends, for he continues to be interested in presenting role playing, ambiguous relationships, and the constant fluctuations and changes in human existence. The fluidity of the situations he creates is beautifully expressed by the glowing electronic lines flashing from side to side and the colors flowing into one another, occasionally merging figure with background or figure with figure as in *Chicaucus,* 1982 (Plate 15). Of the paintings shown, this is the least equivocal, mainly because of its coined title combining the words *Chicago* and *caucus.* The title, together with the fact that it is owned by the State of Illinois and displayed in the recently completed State of Illinois Center, in Chicago, suggests political content. Perhaps it portrays wheeling and dealing.

In contrast to the firm contours and horizontal linear elements in the lower half of *Chicaucus* is the scribblelike line in several of Paschke's paintings, showing some influence of the currently popular Neo-Expressionism. But he is not an artist to have a style imposed upon him. Though he occasionally uses expressionistic scratchlike lines and jagged forms, as in *Dowagiac* (Plate 16) or *Le Sac* (Plate 17), Paschke also explores the opposite in creating some softly brushed impressionistic canvases such as *Towanda* (Plate 18) and *Triandos* (Plate 19), all works of 1983.

As is frequently pointed out, the starting point for a Paschke painting is a photograph drawn from newspapers, magazines, or still shots from films. So completely does he alter these photographs that, when seen side by side with the paintings, they emphasize the extent to which Paschke's creativity soars beyond the often prosaic source of his inspiration. For example, the small background figures in *Radio-TV* were derived from a photograph of a cantor chanting the liturgy, with his arms dramatically raised. Paschke has so totally transformed the figures that their origin is undetectable. Again, though a photograph of Robert de Niro in *True Confessions* was a source for *Meyamo,* 1984 (Plate 21), the power of the painting lies in its carefully calculated color harmonies as well as the massive image of a man whose attention is focused on something beyond our vision. The painting of this shadowy, masked figure has been given an enigmatic title, a verbal pun that sounds like the Spanish *me llamo* ("my name is"), but Paschke stopped short of giving the name. Evading specific identification, perhaps the figure is intended to be Everyman.

Of the 10 works included here, *White Way,* 1985 (Plate 22), makes the stongest confrontation, its subjects staring fixedly at the viewer. The masked figure in the cowboy hat (which could symbolize the tough American frontier) aggressively advances; the second figure, lurking slightly behind him, is equally threatening. The violence that seems to simmer beneath the surface of this work, more overtly expressed in other Paschke paintings, emerges as one of his persistent themes. In recent years its various facets have appeared in the demagoguery of *Gestapo,* 1979; the strangulation in *Violencia,* 1980; the gun toters of *Tropanique,* 1983, and the menacing officers (American or Nazi?) of *Sauganash,* 1983 (Figure 8), and *Kontato,* 1984.

Critics have speculated on the meaning of Paschke's recent paintings: one feels his iconography portrays man's dualistic nature, depersonalization, and isolation, while another says his work is "so personally inflected as to be almost at the limits of description."[6] Paschke, who enjoys the diverse responses his art evokes, has stated: "I attempt to weave a multiplicity of meanings and clues so there is never one correct or absolute interpretation but rather a Rorschach-like series of possibilities."[7] Perhaps the most relevant observation about meaning in Paschke's art is Archibald MacLeish's observation about meaning in poetry:

A Poem should not mean
But be.

Paschke's paintings leave haunting impressions even when they are beyond interpretation. Their imposing imagery, brilliant color, and superb technical execution make Ed Paschke one of the most compelling artists of our day. ◊

Michele Vishny received her PhD in Art History from Northwestern University in 1971. She has lectured in art history at The School of The Art Institute of Chicago, DePaul University, and Northwestern University. A frequent contributor to art journals, Vishny has written on topics ranging from Paul Klee to Red Grooms.

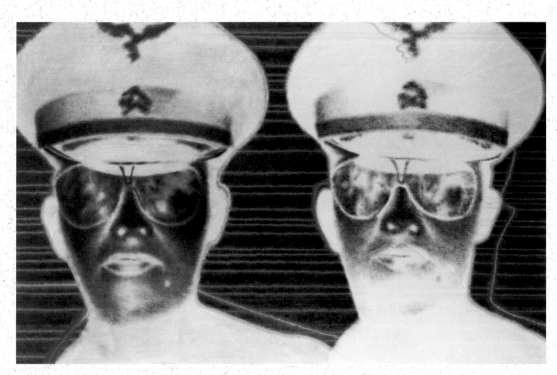

Figure 8. Sauganash, 1983.
Oil on canvas, 46 ×74 inches.
Collection of Ed and Nancy
Paschke.

1. Henri Focillon, *The Life of Forms in Art* (New York: George Wittenborn, 1948), 52.

2. Although Paschke, too, portrayed Marilyn Monroe in three works, these were done later (1970) and convey a content quite different from Warhol's.

3. From a personal interview with the artist, August 13, 1980. For excerpts of this interview, see my article, "An Interview with Ed Paschke," *Arts Magazine* 55 (December 1980): 146-49. Other statements in this essay about Paschke's attitudes toward his work are derived from personal conversations with him.

4. Paschke did paint one headless portrait in 1974 entitled *Bill*, but it is an isolated example. The headless image does not recur until the 1977 works.

5. Polly Ullrich, "Paschke Paints in Warts," *Chicago Sun-Times*, September 4, 1977, sec. 3.

6. See John Yau, "How We Live: The Paintings of Robert Birmelin, Eric Fischl and Ed Paschke," *Artforum* 21 (April 1983): 60-67, and Dennis Adrian in *Ed Paschke: Selected Works 1967-1981* (Chicago: The Renaissance Society, The University of Chicago, 1982), 11.

7. Ed Paschke, "Notes on a Work Process," *New Art Examiner* 11 (January 1984): 5-111.

Ed Paschke was born in Chicago in 1939. He was a Raymond Fellow at The School of The Art Institute of Chicago, where he was awarded a bachelor of fine arts degree in 1961 and, as a Ponte del Arte Fellow, his master of fine arts degree in 1970.

Paschke's art awards include a grant in 1972 from the Cassandra Foundation and the Logan Medal, awarded by The Art Institute of Chicago in 1973. In 1985 he received an Academy Honor from The Academy High School for Performing and Visual Arts in Chicago.

Paschke taught painting at The School of The Art Institute of Chicago from 1974 to 1976 and at Columbia College in Chicago from 1976 to 1978. A faculty member of the Department of Art Theory and Practice at Northwestern University since 1977, Paschke was chair of the department from 1980 to 1985.

1970
Deson-Zaks Gallery, Chicago.
Ed Paschke: New Paintings.

1971
Deson-Zaks Gallery, Chicago.
Hundred Acres Gallery, New York.
Ed Paschke: Paintings.

1972
Deson-Zaks Gallery, Chicago.

1973
Deson-Zaks Gallery, Chicago.
Ed Paschke: New Paintings.
The Richard DeMarco Gallery, Edinburgh, Scotland.

1974
Contemporary Arts Center, Cincinnati. *Ed Paschke.*
Hundred Acres Gallery, New York.

1975
Deson-Zaks Gallery, Chicago.
Ed Paschke: New Paintings and Drawings.
Pyramid Gallery, Washington, D.C.

1976
Galerie Darthea Speyer, Paris.
Marian Locks Gallery, Philadelphia.

1977
Phyllis Kind Gallery, Chicago.

1978
Galerie Darthea Speyer, Paris.
Ed Paschke: Présences.
Phyllis Kind Gallery, New York.

1979
Phyllis Kind Gallery, Chicago.
Phyllis Kind Gallery, New York.

1980
Phyllis Kind Gallery, New York.

1981
Centre d'art contemporain, Geneva, Switzerland.
Galerie Darthea Speyer, Paris.*

1982
Phyllis Kind Gallery, New York.
The Renaissance Society, The University of Chicago. *Ed Paschke: Selected Works 1967-1981.* Traveled to Joslyn Art Museum, Omaha; Contemporary Arts Museum, Houston.*

1983
Galerie Darthea Speyer, Paris.
Phyllis Kind Gallery, Chicago.
Ed Paschke: New Paintings 1983. Traveled to Hewlett Gallery, Carnegie-Mellon University, Pittsburgh; Kalamazoo Institute of Arts, Mich.*

1984
Fuller Goldeen Gallery, San Francisco.
Phyllis Kind Gallery, New York.
Galerie Bonnier, Geneva, Switzerland. *Peintures récentes.*

1986
Phyllis Kind Gallery, New York.

1962
The Art Institute of Chicago. *Sixty-Fifth Annual Exhibition by Artists of Chicago and Vicinity.**

1965
Illinois Institute of Technology, Chicago. *Phalanx 3.*

1966
The Art Institute of Chicago. *Sixty-Ninth Annual Exhibition by Artists of Chicago and Vicinity.**

1967
The Art Institute of Chicago. *Seventieth Annual Exhibition by Artists of Chicago and Vicinity.**
Illinois Arts Council, Chicago. *Six Illinois Painters 67/69: Arcilesi, Ito, Lanyon, Paschke, Rosofsky, Wirsum.* State-wide tour through 1969 under the auspices of the Illinois Arts Council.

1968
Hyde Park Art Center, Chicago. *Nonplussed Some.*
Museum of Contemporary Art, Chicago. *Violence in Recent American Art.**

1969
Hyde Park Art Center, Chicago. *Nonplussed Some – Some More.*
Museum of Contemporary Art, Chicago. *Don Baum Sez "Chicago Needs Famous Artists."*
The Art Institute of Chicago. *Seventy-Second Annual Exhibition by Artists of Chicago and Vicinity.**
Institute of Contemporary Art, University of Pennsylvania, Philadelphia. *The Spirit of the Comics.**
Museum of Contemporary Art, Chicago. *Art by Telephone.*
Whitney Museum of American Art, New York. *Human Concern/Personal Torment: The Grotesque in American Art.* Traveled through 1970 to University Art Museum, University of California, Berkeley.*

1970

Hyde Park Art Center, Chicago. *Marriage Chicago Style.*

Indianapolis Museum of Art. *Painting and Sculpture Today.*

San Francisco Art Institute. *Serplus Slop from the Windy City.* Traveled to Sacramento State College Art Gallery.

1971

Hyde Park Art Center, Chicago. *Chicago Antigua.*

Barcelona, Spain. *III Bienial Internacional en Las Bellas Artes.*

1972

Indianapolis Museum of Art. *Painting and Sculpture Today.*

Museum of Contemporary Art, Chicago. *Chicago Imagist Art.* Traveled to New York Cultural Center.*

1973

Whitney Museum of American Art, New York. *1973 Biennial Exhibition.*

The Art Institute of Chicago. *Seventy-Fourth Annual Exhibition by Artists of Chicago and Vicinity.**

Museu de Arte, São Paulo, Brazil. *XII Bienal de São Paulo: Made in Chicago.*

1974

The Bergman Gallery, The University of Chicago. *The Chicago Style – Painting.**

Krannert Art Museum, University of Illinois, Champaign. *Contemporary American Painting and Sculpture.**

The Art Institute of Chicago. *Seventy First American Exhibition.**

The Art Institute of Chicago. *Seventy-Fifth Annual Exhibition by Artists of Chicago and Vicinity.**

National Museum of American Art (formerly National Collection of Fine Arts), Washington, D.C. *Made in Chicago.* Traveled through 1975 to Museum of Contemporary Art, Chicago.*

1975

Moore College of Art Gallery, Philadelphia. *North, East, West, South, and Middle: An Exhibition of Contemporary American Drawings.* Traveled through 1976 to Pratt Graphics Center, New York; Corcoran Gallery of Art, Washington, D.C.; Fort Worth Art Museum; La Jolla Museum of Contemporary Art, Calif.*

1976

Hyde Park Art Center, Chicago. *Hyde Park Center Retrospective Exhibition: Historic Panoramic Abra Cadabra.*

The School of The Art Institute of Chicago. *Visions – Painting and Sculpture: Distinguished Alumni 1945 to the Present.**

Grand Palais, Paris. *FIAC '76: 3eme Foire internationale d'art contemporain.*

Illinois Arts Council, Chicago. *Koffler Foundation Collection.* State-wide tour through 1978 under the auspices of the Illinois Arts Council.*

Crocker Art Museum (formerly E.B. Crocker Art Gallery), Sacramento. *The Chicago Connection.* Traveled through 1977 to Newport Harbor Art Museum, Newport Beach, Calif.; Phoenix Art Museum; Memphis Brooks Museum of Art; Memorial Art Gallery, University of Rochester, N.Y.

1977

Madison Art Center, Wis. *Contemporary Figurative Painting in the Midwest: An Invitational Exhibition.**

Museum of Contemporary Art, Chicago. *A View of a Decade.*

University Gallery of Fine Art, Ohio State University, Columbus. *Chicago '77.*

1978

The University of Michigan Museum of Art, Ann Arbor. *Chicago: The City and Its Artists 1945-1978.**

University of Northern Iowa Museum, Cedar Falls. *Contemporary Chicago Painters.**

The Art Institute of Chicago. *Works on Paper: Seventy-Seventh Annual Exhibition by Artists of Chicago and Vicinity.**

Grand Palais, Paris. *Salon de mai.*

1979

Grand Palais, Paris. *International exposition d'art.*

National Museum of American Art (formerly National Collection of Fine Arts), Washington, D.C. *Chicago Currents: The Koffler Foundation Collection of the National Collection of Fine Arts.*

The Art Institute of Chicago. *100 Artists 100 Years: Alumni of The School of The Art Institute of Chicago. Centennial Exhibition.**

1980

The Ackland Art Museum, University of North Carolina, Chapel Hill. *Some Recent Art from Chicago.**

The David and Alfred Smart Gallery, The University of Chicago. *Master Prints from Landfall Press.**

Mary and Leigh Block Gallery, Northwestern University, Evanston, Ill. *Collaborations.**

The Mayor Gallery, London. *Six Artists from Chicago.*

Camden Arts Centre, London. *Who Chicago? An Exhibition of Contemporary Imagists.* Traveled through 1982 to Ceolfrith Gallery, Sunderland Arts Centre, England; Third Eye Gallery, Glasgow, Scotland; Scottish National Gallery of Modern Art, Edinburgh; Museum of Fine Arts, Boston.*

1981

Whitney Museum of American Art, New York. *1981 Biennial Exhibition.*

Cleveland Museum of Art. *Contemporary Artists.**

Newport Harbor Art Museum, Newport Beach, Calif. *Inside/Out: Self Beyond Likeness.* Traveled to Joslyn Art Museum, Omaha; Portland Art Museum, Oregon.*

The Art Institute of Chicago. *Prints and Multiples: Seventy-Ninth Annual Exhibition by Artists of Chicago and Vicinity.**

1982

The Pace Gallery, New York. *From Chicago.**

Indianapolis Museum of Art. *Painting and Sculpture Today.*

Museum of Contemporary Art, Chicago. *Selections from the Dennis Adrian Collection.**

Whitney Museum of American Art, New York. *Focus on the Figure: 20 Years.**

1983

Rudolf Zwirner Gallery, Cologne, West Germany. *Group Show.*

Galerie Bonnier, Geneva, Switzerland. *Gladys Nilsson, Jim Nutt, Ed Paschke, Suellen Rocca, Karl Wirsum.**

Phyllis Kind Gallery, New York and Chicago. *Dialect ≠ Dialectic: A Group Show of Artists with Complex Individual Vocabularies.*

ARC Gallery, Chicago. *Art on the Edge.*

Artemesia Gallery, Chicago. *Looking at Women: Images of Women by Contemporary Artists.*

Archer M. Huntington Art Gallery, University of Texas, Austin. *New American Painting: A Tribute to James and Mari Michener.*

Rhona Hoffman Gallery, Chicago. *Artists Call Against U.S. Intervention in Central America and the Caribbean.*

1984

Museum of Contemporary Art, Chicago. *10 Years of Collecting at the MCA.**

The Museum of Modern Art, New York. *An International Survey of Recent Painting and Sculpture.**

Hirshhorn Museum and Sculpture Garden, Washington, D.C. *Content: A Contemporary Focus 1974-1984.**

1985

The Corcoran Gallery of Art, Washington, D.C. *The 39th Biennial Exhibition of Contemporary American Painting.* Traveled to Mary and Leigh Block Gallery, Northwestern University, Evanston, Ill.; The Butler Institute of American Art, Youngstown, Ohio; Contemporary Arts Center, Cincinnati.*

Henry Art Gallery, University of Washington, Seattle. *Sources of Light: Contemporary American Luminism.**

Whitney Museum of American Art, New York. *1985 Biennial Exhibition.*

The Renaissance Society, The University of Chicago. *Chicago White Sox Baseball Card Show.*

1986

The Art Institute of Chicago. *Seventy-Fifth American Exhibition.**

*A catalogue or brochure accompanied the exhibition.

Selected Bibliography

Books and Catalogues

Ann Arbor, The University of Michigan Museum of Art. *Chicago: The City and Its Artists 1945-1978*. 1978.

Cedar Falls, University of Northern Iowa Museum. *Contemporary Chicago Painters*. 1978. Essay by Sanford Sivitz Shaman.

Chapel Hill, Ackland Art Museum, University of North Carolina. *Some Recent Art from Chicago*. 1980. Essay and interview by Katharine Lee Keefe.

Chicago, The Art Institute of Chicago. *100 Artists 100 Years: Alumni of The School of The Art Institute of Chicago. Centennial Exhibition*. 1979. Essay by Katharine Kuh.

Chicago, Museum of Contemporary Art. *Chicago Imagist Art*. 1972. Essay by Franz Schulze.

_____. *Selections from the Dennis Adrian Collection*. 1982.

_____. *Violence in Recent American Art*. 1969. Essay by Robert Glauber.

Chicago, The Renaissance Society, The University of Chicago. *Ed Paschke: Selected Works 1967-1981*. 1982. Essays by Dennis Adrian, Linda L. Cathcart, Holliday T. Day, and Richard Flood.

Chicago, The School of The Art Institute of Chicago. *Visions – Painting and Sculpture: Distinguished Alumni 1945 to the Present*. 1976. Essay by Dennis Adrian.

Chicago, The School of The Art Institute of Chicago, Video Data Bank. *Profile: Ed Paschke*. 1983. Produced by Lyn Blumenthal and Kate Horsefield.

Geneva, Switzerland, Galerie Bonnier. *Gladys Nilsson, Jim Nutt, Ed Paschke, Suellen Rocca, Karl Wirsum*. 1983.

London, Camden Arts Centre. *Who Chicago? An Exhibition of Contemporary Imagists*. 1981. Essays by Dennis Adrian, Russell Bowman, and Roger Brown.

Lucie-Smith, Edward. *American Art Now*. New York: William Morrow and Company, Inc., 1985.

Madison, Wis., Madison Art Center. *Contemporary Figurative Painting in the Midwest: An Invitational Exhibition*. 1977. Essay by Gibson Byrd.

Newport Beach, Calif., Newport Harbor Art Museum. *Inside/Out: Self Beyond Likeness*. 1981. Essays by Lynn Gamwell and Victoria Kogan.

New York, The Museum of Modern Art. *An International Survey of Recent Painting and Sculpture*. 1984. Essay by Kynaston McShine.

New York, The Pace Gallery. *From Chicago*. 1982. Essay by Russell Bowman.

New York, Whitney Museum of American Art. *Human Concern/Personal Torment: The Grotesque in American Art*. 1969. Essay by Robert Doty.

Paris, Galerie Darthea Speyer. *Ed Paschke*. 1981. Essay by James A. Speyer.

Philadelphia, Institute of Contemporary Art, University of Pennsylvania. *The Spirit of the Comics*. 1969. Essay by Joan Siegfried.

Philadelphia, Moore College of Art Gallery. *North, East, West, South, and Middle: An Exhibition of Contemporary American Drawings*. 1975. Essay by Peter Plagens.

Pittsburgh, Hewlett Gallery, Carnegie-Mellon University. *Ed Paschke: New Paintings 1983*. 1983. Essay by Elaine A. King.

Sacramento, E.B. Crocker Art Gallery (now Crocker Art Museum). *The Chicago Connection*. 1976. Essay by Wilma Beaty Cox.

Schulze, Franz. *Fantastic Images: Chicago Art Since 1945*. Chicago: Follett Publishing Company, 1972.

Schwartz, Barry. *The New Humanism. Art in a Time of Change*. New York and Washington: Praeger Publishers, 1974.

Seattle, Henry Art Gallery, University of Washington. *Sources of Light: Contemporary American Luminism*. 1985. Essay by Harvey West.

Washington, D.C., The Corcoran Gallery of Art. *The 39th Biennial Exhibition of Contemporary American Painting*. 1985. Essay by Lisa Lyons.

Washington, D.C., Hirshhorn Museum and Sculpture Garden. *Content: A Contemporary Focus 1974-1984*. 1984. Essays by Howard N. Fox, Miranda McClintic, and Phyllis Rosenzweig.

Washington, D.C., National Collection of Fine Arts (now National Museum of American Art). *Made in Chicago*. 1974. Essay by Whitney Halstead.

Articles and Reviews

Adams, Brook. "The Progress of Ed Paschke." *Art in America* 70 (October 1982): 114-122.

Adrian, Dennis. "And Now, Theater Sees his 'Hell'." *Chicago Daily News* (July 29-30, 1972): Panorama/5.

_____. "Drawings of the '70s: A Many-styled Show." *Chicago Daily News* (March 12-13, 1977): Panorama/12-13.

Allen, Jane and Derek Guthrie. "Stripping the Strippers, An Evening with Ed Paschke." *New Art Examiner* 1 (December 1973): 3.

Artner, Alan. "MCA Rounds Up Dennis Adrian's 'Maverick' Herd." *Chicago Tribune* (February 7, 1982): 6/8-9.

_____. "New Showings Spotlight the Chicago Artists." *Chicago Tribune* (October 23, 1977): 6/14.

_____. "Paschke Show: 34 Eye-openers from a Chicago Master." *Chicago Tribune* (March 14, 1982): 6/15.

_____. "Paschke's Paintings at Phyllis Kind Clothe Image in Distorted-Video Mask." *Chicago Tribune* (September 23, 1983): 5/18.

_____. "So Long, Greenbergian Formalism, Here Come Meaning and Experience." *Chicago Tribune* (April 24, 1983): 6/13.

Baker, Kenneth. "Reviews: Ed Paschke at Phyllis Kind." *Art in America* 73 (February 1985): 139-140.

Beckley, Bill. "Reviews and Previews: Ed Paschke." *Art News* 70 (April 1971): 20, 66.

Blecha, Karen. "Success Hasn't Changed the Kid in Ed Paschke." *Herald*, Chicago (April 20, 1973): 4/1.

Blinderman, Barry. "Ed Paschke: Reflections and Digressions on 'The Body Electric'." *Arts Magazine* 56 (May 1982): 130-131.

Bonesteel, Michael. "Ed Paschke at Phyllis Kind Gallery." *Artforum* 22 (January 1984): 81-82.

_____. "Hairy, Scary, Odd and Daring: 'Selections from the Dennis Adrian Collection at the Museum of Contemporary Art'." *Reader*, Chicago (February 12, 1982): 34, 36.

_____. "The 39th Corcoran Biennial: The Death Knell of Regionalism?" *Art in America* 73 (October 1985): 31-37.

Bowman, Russell. "Ed Paschke." *Arts Magazine* 53 (October 1978): 14.

Byrne-Dodge, Teresa. "CAM Show of Paschke Works Opens." *Houston Post* (August 22, 1982): 14AA.

Cavalier, Barbara. "Reviews: From Chicago." *Arts Magazine* 56 (March 1982): 26.

Day, Holly T. "Ed Paschke at Phyllis Kind." *Art in America* 66 (March-April 1978): 144.

Edelman, Robert G. "Ed Paschke: Selected Works, 1967-1981." *New Art Examiner* 9 (May 1982): 19.

Elliott, David. "Chicago is Enjoying its Own Eclecticism." *Art News* 81 (May 1982): 90-94.

————. "Collector Adrian: A Gambler Who Loves Wild Cards." *Chicago Sun-Times* (February 14, 1982): 5/7.

Flood, Richard. "Reviews, New York: Ed Paschke." *Artforum* 19 (February 1981): 73-74.

Frueh, Joanna. "Chicago's Emotional Realists." *Artforum* 17 (September 1978): 41-47.

Gedo, Mary Mathews. "Dennis Adrian Collection." *Arts Magazine* 56 (April 1982): 9.

————. "Interconnections: A Study of Chicago Style Relationships in Painting." *Arts Magazine* 58 (September 1983): 92-97.

Glowen, Ron. "Concentrating on Light." *Artweek* 16 (May 4, 1985): 5.

Hachett, Regina. "Luminists Shed Light on their Art Form." *Seattle Post-Intelligencer* (April 4, 1985): C8.

Halstead, Whitney. "Chicago." *Artforum* 6 (Summer 1968): 63-65.

Hanson, Henry. "Paschke Mini-retrospective." *Chicago* (April 1982): 128.

Harris, Susan A. "Reviews: Ed Paschke." *Arts Magazine* 59 (November 1984): 42.

Haydon, Harold. "Easel Does It. Painterly Paschke Sets up Tensions." *Chicago Sun-Times* (October 23, 1977): 5/17.

————. "Five 'Nonplussed' Artists Exhibit Striking Works." *Chicago Sun-Times* (February 25, 1968): 5/6.

Heartney, Eleanor. "Reviews: Ed Paschke." *Arts Magazine* 59 (November 1984): 36.

Homisak, William. "Reviews: Ed Paschke." *New Art Examiner* 11 (January 1984): 16.

Hoxie, Elizabeth. "Ed Paschke." *New Art Examiner* 7 (December 1979): 13.

Hughes, Robert. "Midwestern Eccentrics." *Time* 99 (June 12, 1972): 52-59.

Januszczak, Waldemar. "Chicago Defies you to Like its Art." *Guardian*, London (December 17, 1980): 10.

Kalil, Suzy. "Art: 'Ed Paschke Selected Works'." *Houston Post* (September 12, 1982): 25AA.

Kozloff, Max. "Inwardness: Chicago Art Since 1945." *Artforum* 11 (October 1972): 51-55.

Larson, Kay. "Caws and Effect." *Village Voice*, New York (December 31, 1979): 66.

Leslie, Rich. "A Meditation on Mediation: Paschke's New Work." *New Art Examiner* 2 (March 1984): 11.

Lyon, Christopher. "By Art Possessed." *Chicago* (May 1984): 174-80, 200.

————. "Coming in from the Cold." *Chicago* (May 1984): 156-69; 196, 198.

————. "Gallery Tripping: Ed Paschke's Signal Achievements." *Reader*, Chicago (March 5, 1982): 6.

Micha, René. "Reviews: Ed Paschke." *Art International* 21 (January 1977): 43.

Morrison, C.L. "Chicago Dialectic." *Artforum* 16 (February 1978): 32-39.

Moufarrege, Nicolas A. "Intoxication: April 9, 1983." *Arts Magazine* 57 (April 1983): 70-76.

Olegarz, Harold. "Reviews: Ed Paschke." *Arts Magazine* 53 (November 1978): 29.

Paschke, Ed. "Speakeasy." *New Art Examiner* 9 (February 1982): 3.

Raynor, Vivian. "Art: Ed Paschke." *New York Times* (October 5, 1984): C28.

Russell, John. "Art: Ed Paschke." *New York Times* (May 27, 1983): C19.

————. "'The Hairy Who' and the Other Messages from Chicago." *New York Times* (January 31, 1982): C29.

Russell Taylor, John. "The Arts: Painting to Challenge the Strongest of Stomachs." *Times*, London (December 23, 1980): 7.

Schjeldahl, Peter. "Art: The Hallelujah Trail." *Village Voice*, New York (March 18, 1981): 77.

————. "Chicagoization: Some Second Thoughts on the Second City." *New Art Examiner* 12 (May 1985): 28-32.

————. "Letter from Chicago." *Art in America* 64 (July-August 1976): 52-58.

Schulze, Franz. "Art News in Chicago." *Art News* 70 (November 1971): 48-55.

————. "Chicago: Bigger and Livelier but..." *Art News* 78 (February 1979): 40-45.

————. "Paschke, Master of Monsters." *Chicago Daily News* (October 1-2, 1977): Panorama/14-15.

————. "So You Think That's Just a Shoe?" *Chicago Daily News* (November 27-28, 1971): Panorama/13.

Tully, Judd. "The Chicago Art Scene." *Flash Art International* 103 (Summer 1981): 23-26.

Upshaw, Reagan. "Kind Stable Sets Pace in Manhattan." *New Art Examiner* 9 (May 1982): 11.

Vishny, Michele. "An Interview with Ed Paschke." *Arts Magazine* 55 (December 1980): 146-49.

Wells, Daniel. "Paschke's Childhood Key to His Paintings." *Chicago Tribune* (August 16, 1970): 5/12.

Yau, John. "How We Live: The Paintings of Robert Birmelin, Eric Fischl and Ed Paschke." *Artforum* 21 (April 1983): 60-67.

Ed Paschke

13

Radio–TV 1977 and 1980
Oil on canvas
80 × 102 inches
Collection of The Northern
Trust Company

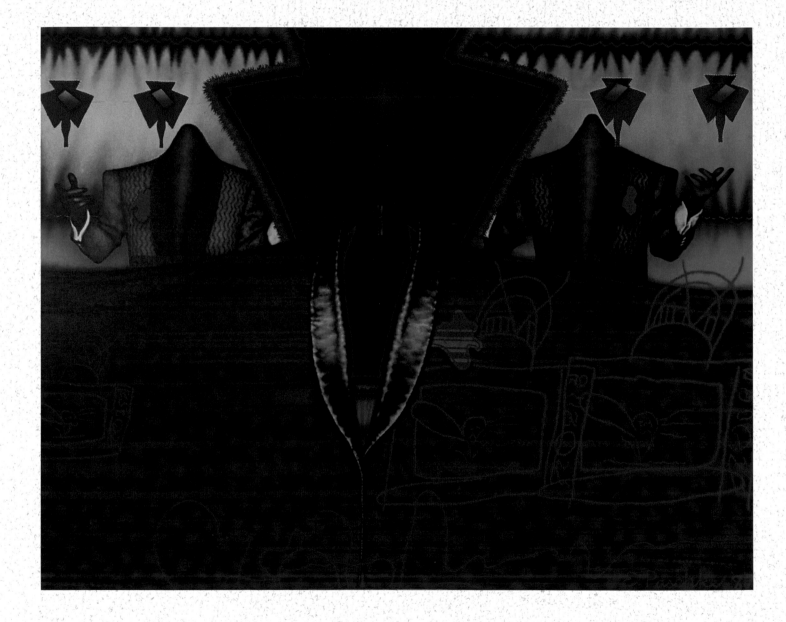

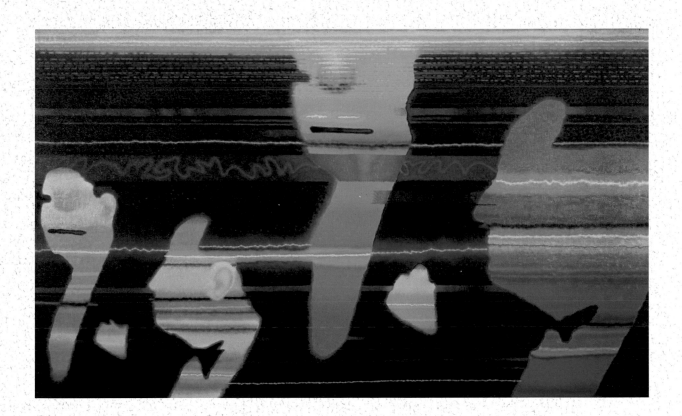

14

Delamar 1981
Oil on canvas
50 × 84 inches
Collection of
Orrin and Joanne Scheff

Chicaucus 1982
Oil on canvas
80 × 96 inches
Illinois Collection,
State of Illinois Center

16

Dowagiac 1983
Oil on canvas
48 × 60 inches
Collection of Steven Berkowitz

17

Le Sac 1983
Oil on canvas
48 × 72 inches
Collection of Lois and Bruce Berry

18

Towanda 1983
Oil on canvas
54 × 80 inches
Collection of Robert H. Bergman

19

Triandos 1983
Oil on canvas
54 × 80 inches
Collection of William H. Plummer

20

Dos Egos 1984
Oil on canvas
80×96 inches
Courtesy of Phyllis Kind Gallery,
Chicago and New York

21

Meyamo 1984
Oil on canvas
72 × 68 inches
Collection of
Dr. and Mrs. Larry Milner

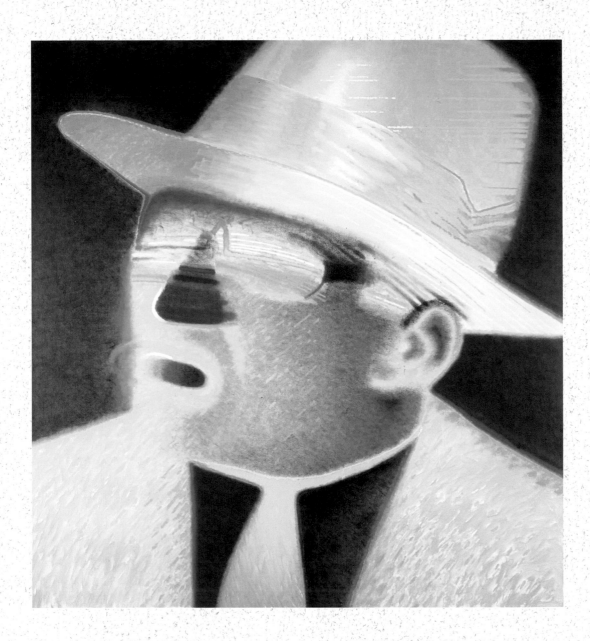

22

White Way 1985
Oil on canvas
50 × 80 inches
Collection of
Doris and Irwin Esko

James Valerio

by John Arthur

One of the more fascinating developments in the recent history of contemporary Realism has been James Valerio's move from the periphery of Photorealism to a position of major significance in less than a decade.

In the early 1970s, discussions of Photorealism centered on painting as simulacrum, the mechanical or photographic means of establishing an image, and the primary identification of individual artists by subject. The import of these factors has diminished considerably, but they were central issues at that time. James Valerio was known to those following developments in Realism and Photorealism, and his technical virtuosity and pictorial ambitions were in place by the early 1970s. But the narrative ambiguities and frank sexuality of his paintings flew in the face of all who had developed an appetite for other artists' emotionally neutral, obsessive examinations of manufactured objects. While the explicit rendering of Detroit chrome, glass, and steel, or the overwhelming banality of urban architecture attracted critics and collectors and could be aesthetically justified as replication of a replica and an extension of Pop, Valerio's emphatic scrutiny of the sagging breasts and flabby thighs of a less-than-ideal nude participating in an obviously contrived situation, such as Four Models and a Chicken, 1975 (Figure 1), repelled with equal force.

The marvelous incongruity of the coquettish, over-the-hill Honey Bun, 1974, nude before her dresser (which reappears in Pat Combing Her Hair, 1983), seated on a diaphanous robe, with dainty red slippers and scattered roses on the floor, seems to parody the glossy centerfold depictions of femininity and to mock voyeurism. Simultaneously, the swollen, sagging flesh that delineates the effects of time, gravity, and overindulgence refers back to Into the World There Came a Soul Called Ida, 1928, by Chicago artist Ivan Albright.

This Chicago connection provides a clue to the distinctly different sources of Valerio's work. He studied at Wright Junior College with Seymour Rosofsky, and with Ray Yoshida at The School of The Art Institute. He was also familiar with the works of Robert Barnes and James McGarrell, who were extremely influential in the Midwest in the 1960s.

That all painting is artifice is tacitly understood; "Ceci n'est pas une pipe." Valerio's emphatic reminder, via the theatricality and the implicit improbability of his earlier images, such as Four Models and a Chicken and Swan Lake and Signorelli's Lament, was an audacious ploy; it was at precisely the same time that other painters were not only insistent on minimizing the evidence of their hand, but also were withdrawing into an interpretive neutrality. Valerio's emotional tone, the unromanticized sexuality of his subjects, and the lack of narrative probity in his paintings were extremely disconcerting to viewers.

James Valerio acknowledges that these early paintings were a bit "forced," and they are certainly some of the least ingratiating images in contemporary art. But, when the more blatantly surreal aspects were toned down, as in Gail, 1977, or shifted to a more palatable allegory, such as Paul's Magic, 1977, his paintings acquired a more sympathetic audience.

Gail is a full-length portrait. The attractive model, clothed in and surrounded by an assortment of elaborately patterned fabrics, makes direct eye contact with the viewer. It is an opulent painting, with only minor enigmatic traces: three goldfish float in the air above her, and the slightly menacing foliage of a tropical plant rises beyond the window. In Paul's Magic (Figure 2), a magician passes a woman through a levitating hoop, while Paul (the artist's son) releases a bag of exotic fish and birds in the foreground. The fish move through the air as naturally as the birds do. The incident unfolds in a barren, burnt-out forest.

Figure 1. Four Models and a Chicken, 1975. Oil on canvas, 68½×79 inches. Collection of the artist.

Figure 2. Paul's Magic, 1977.
Oil on canvas, 94 ×108 inches.
Collection of Mr. and Mrs.
Marvin Gerstin.

Figure 3. Still Life #1, 1978.
Oil on canvas, 95 ×85½ inches.
Private collection.

The invitation in the summer of 1978 to produce a major painting for *The Big Still Life* exhibition at New York's Allan Frumkin Gallery was, by all accounts, the turning point in James Valerio's career. This exhibition was to remove him from the uncomfortable and inappropriate context of Photo-realism and place him in the notable company of Alfred Leslie, Jack Beal, Paul Georges, James McGarrell, Paul Wonner, Sondra Freckelton, and others, while giving him high visibility in a distinguished New York gallery. In addition, it required him to address thoughtfully the venerable tradition of still life painting, an avenue he had not previously explored. Valerio's first painting for the exhibition, *Still Life #1*, 1978 (Figure 3), was considered more of an interior than a still life, for it placed a strong emphasis on the figure of a woman seen from the back, and thus was not quite appropriate for the theme of the exhibition.

With a pressing deadline, he proceeded with the monumental *Still Life #2*, 1978 (Plate 23; Figure 4, detail). This extravagant, virtuoso painting refers to those opulent 17th-century Dutch productions such as the table and banquet pieces by de Heem and Kalf, but there is an understated hallucinatory and animistic intensity that recalls Zurbaran and Sanchez Cotan. All of the objects are slightly larger than life, and their clarity and color are emphasized over chiaroscuro and tone. The green wall that serves as a chromatic backdrop for the still life was, in fact, a plasterboard garage wall, which is evidence of Valerio's ability to depart convincingly from his source material. This pivotal painting, one of the most striking pieces in an illustrious and influential exhibition, greatly expanded the painter's audience. *Still Life #2* has been one of the most widely exhibited and frequently reproduced works in contemporary Realism.

Figure 4. Still Life #2, detail.

Figure 5. Self-Portrait, *detail*.

Since 1978, James Valerio has produced an astonishing number of ambitious and equally memorable paintings and drawings. *Card Trick*, 1979 (Plate 24), and *Checkers*, 1980 (Plate 25), were Valerio's first excursions into genre painting, and both contain Dutch references. *Card Trick*, which had its germination in a newspaper photograph of a murdered mobster, was composed from an assortment of large transparencies of groups of figures. The baroque light (the only connection to the news photo), which articulates the figures and focuses the composition, was improvised by the painter.

Checkers depicts the artist's wife and son in their basement game room. Like *Paul's Magic and Card Trick*, a minor incident provides a psychological connector, serves as the narrative fulcrum, and suspends a fleeting moment (as do Vermeer's *The Love Letter, The Milkmaid,* and *Woman with Balance*) into an act that will never be completed. Its composition is more like that of *Officer with a Laughing Girl*, including the lenslike distortion of the relative scale of the figures and the checkerboard that mirrors in miniature the gridded floors that define the space of so many 17th-century Dutch paintings. The oversized fern, stationed at the far side of the table like a third participant, is similar to that earlier, ominous foliage outside the window in *Gail*.

Almost every figurative artist eventually turns to the mirror as a means of self-inventory. In Valerio's contemplative *Self-Portrait*, 1981 (Plate 27), the painting is composed with the rigid symmetry of an icon, but it is tipped slightly off balance by an easel and stepladder on the left. The portrait is set during the closing minutes of the last hour of the day, a time that seems to amplify contemplation. On the cluttered, glass-topped table are the tools for recording those interior thoughts: notepad, pencil, pen, sable brushes, and ruler (Figure 5, detail). A clock stabilizes the time, a child's block indicates the past, and the telephone and letter connect the scene with the world outside. On another level, there is the ominous nuclear symbol of four minutes to midnight, a replica of a submarine, and a glowing red light on the telephone. Beyond the figure, the room fades into a dark infinity of space.

Pat Combing Her Hair, 1983 (Plate 28), evolved from an earlier drawing of the same title (Figure 6). The rendering focuses on the mirror reflection of the painter's wife, which is pushed into the upper left half of the composition. She wears a dark, elaborately patterned jacket, and an assortment of toiletries in front of her is reflected in the mirror. On the left, the diffused outline of the brush and several objects on the dressing table are seen through the pulled swirl of Pat's hair. This elaborate brocade of lights and darks recalls, technically, the highly finished conté drawings of Charles Sheeler. Its ambience, however, is closer to Vuillard's 1930s' paintings of glowing, self-absorbed women in interiors such as *Le boudoir au voile de Gênes*, or *Une dame sous la lampe*.

While the drawing *Pat Combing Her Hair* is repeated in the painting almost exactly (the school photograph of Paul has been updated and moved to the right of the mirror), there is an emphatic intensification of mood with the shift of color, and the perimeters are broadened to include the interior. Pat is seen full length in front of a dark green dresser from, perhaps, the interior of a closet. The scale of the foreground objects is extremely exaggerated: the jewelry box is much larger than the dresser, hangers and a blouse dwarf the figure, and a geranium fills the left side of the painting. The articles are reminiscent in size of Hitchcock's gargantuan telephone (*Dial M for Murder*), and painted in shades of green against an earth-toned interior, they recall the artifice of the painted objects in Antonioni's movie *Red Desert*. These highly cinematic devices, such as the juxtaposition of scale and manipulations of color, are carefully considered means of controlling the nuance of the painting.

The same strategies are carried into *Night Fires*, 1984 (Plate 29), amongst the most beautiful and memorable works in contemporary Realism. The foreground of the painting, which is a veritable feast for the eye, seems partly an homage to those floral extravagances by de Heem and van Huysum, and in part a reference to Degas' *Woman with Chrysanthemums*. Beyond the table, Pat sleeps on a chintz-covered sofa. Again, Valerio incorporates the exaggeration of relative scale between the still life and the figure. The background opens into the dark night, which is punctuated by the flickering remains of a dying fire.

The most recent work included here, *Still Life with Tomatoes*, 1985 (Plate 30), recalls the earlier tableau *Still Life #2*. It shares the same frontality, descriptive clarity, and emphatic color. Also, there is avoidance of a dominant compositional center; the use of chromatic punctuation points is favored instead. And, once again, the background withdraws into a recess of infinite shadow.

While disconcertingly overstated, Valerio's earlier paintings more closely correspond with the ambiguous imagery of James McGarrell and Robert Barnes. Also, there are striking parallels with the photographs of Les Krims: the recurrent use of that fleshy, middle-aged model, immortalized in the Dorian Gray-like *Honey Bun,* and the numerous acerbic portraits of the photographer's mother; of those leaping cats, suspended in mid-air before the naked dancers in the painting *Reclining Dancer,* 1978, and in a photograph by Krims.

Other than the astonishing lucidity of his images, there is very little linkage with Photorealism in Valerio's work; all of Valerio's paintings are assimilations derived from transparencies, drawings, and direct observations, rather than mere replications of photographic source material. Paintings such as *Checkers* and *Card Trick* can be regarded as genre subjects, and *Still Life #2* and *Still Life on Bedspread* (Plate 26) mark Valerio's convergence with contemporary Realism while clarifying his aesthetic heritage. But it is in *Self-Portrait, Pat Combing Her Hair, Night Fires,* and others that the painter seems to have found his true center. These enigmatic images add up to a psychologically charged total that is more than the isolated meanings of their individual parts. Their residue lingers in one's memory with astonishing clarity and intensity. ◇

John Arthur is an independent curator who has authored four books and numerous articles and catalogues devoted to contemporary American Realism. Most recently he curated American Realism: The Precise Image, *a major exhibition of contemporary Realist painters that toured Japan in 1985.*

Notes

Among the sources consulted in preparation of this essay are:

Arthur, John. *Realist Drawings and Watercolors*. Boston: New York Graphic Society, 1980.

————. *Realists at Work*. New York: Watson-Guptill Publications, 1983.

Martin, J. "A Conversation with James Valerio." *Allan Frumkin Gallery Newsletter* 13 (Fall 1981): 1-3.

New York, Allan Frumkin Gallery. *James Valerio: New Paintings and Drawings*. 1983.

James Valerio was born in Chicago in 1938. As a student at The School of The Art Institute of Chicago, Valerio received many awards: the Daniel D. Van der Grift Scholarship, 1964; Louis Alexander Scholarship, 1965; The School of The Art Institute Scholarship, 1966; and the Anne Louise Raymond Foreign Traveling Fellowship, 1968. He received a bachelor of fine arts degree with honors in 1966 and a master of fine arts degree with honors in 1968.

Valerio was assistant professor at Rock Valley College, Rockford, Illinois, from 1968 to 1970. He was associate professor at the University of California at Los Angeles from 1970 to 1978 and at Cornell University from 1979 to 1982. He joined the Department of Art Theory and Practice at Northwestern University as a full professor in 1985. In 1985 he also received an Artist's Fellowship from the National Endowment for the Arts.

Figure 6. Pat Combing Her Hair, 1981. Pencil on paper, 29½ × 41½ inches. Collection of Herbert and Ann Gold.

One-Person Exhibitions

1971
Gerald John Hayes Gallery, Los Angeles.

1972
Gerald John Hayes Gallery, Los Angeles.

1973
Tucson Art Center, Arizona.

1974
Michael Walls Gallery, New York.

1977
John Berggruen Gallery, San Francisco.

1981
Frumkin and Struve Gallery, Chicago.

1983
Delaware Art Museum, Wilmington.

Allan Frumkin Gallery, New York. *James Valerio: New Paintings and Drawings.**

1984
Frumkin and Struve Gallery, Chicago.

Selected Group Exhibitions

1969
The Art Institute of Chicago. *Seventy-Second Annual Exhibition by Artists of Chicago and Vicinity.**

Theodore Lyman Wright Art Center, Beloit College, Wis. *Twelfth Annual Beloit and Vicinity Show.**

1970
Theodore Lyman Wright Art Center, Beloit College, Wis. *Thirteenth Annual Beloit and Vicinity Show.**

1971
Indianapolis Museum of Art. *Painting and Sculpture Today.**

Long Beach Museum of Art, Calif. *Ninth Annual Southern California Exhibition.**

Long Beach Museum of Art, Calif. *American Portraits Old and New.**

Western New Mexico University Museum, Silver City. *Graphics 71 National Print and Drawing Exhibition.**

1973
De Cordova and Dana Museum and Park, Lincoln, Mass. *The Super-Realist Vision.**

Los Angeles Municipal Art Gallery. *Separate Realities: Developments in California Representational Painting and Sculpture.**

1974
Akron Art Museum. *Selections in Contemporary Realism.**

1975
John Berggruen Gallery, San Francisco. *Realist Painting in California.*

Louis K. Meisel Gallery, New York. *Watercolors and Drawings: American Realists.*

The Los Angeles Institute of Contemporary Art. *Current Concerns, 2.*

1976
Frederick S. Wight Art Gallery, University of California, Los Angeles. *Eighteen UCLA Faculty Artists.**

1977
San Francisco Museum of Modern Art. *Painting and Sculpture in California: The Modern Era.* Traveled to the National Museum of American Art (formerly the National Collection of Fine Arts), Washington, D.C.*

1979
Allan Frumkin Gallery, New York. *The Big Still Life.* Traveled to The University of Virginia Art Museum, Charlottesville; Boston University Art Gallery.*

Albuquerque Museum of Art. *Reflections of Realism.**

Anderson Gallery, Virginia Commonwealth University, Richmond. *Three Bravura Painters of the Human Figure.*

Memorial Art Gallery, University of Rochester, N.Y. *Uncommon Visions.**

Herbert F. Johnson Museum, Cornell University, Ithaca, N.Y. *Art Faculty Exhibition.*

1980
Herbert F. Johnson Museum, Cornell University, Ithaca, N.Y. *Art Faculty Exhibition.*

Philbrook Art Center, Tulsa, Okla. *Realism/Photorealism.**

1981
Allan Frumkin Gallery, New York. *Narrative Painting.**

Newport Harbor Art Museum, Newport Beach, Calif. *Inside/Out: Self Beyond Likeness.* Traveled to Joslyn Art Museum, Omaha; Portland Art Museum, Oregon.*

San Antonio Museum of Art. *Real, Really Real, Super Real.* Traveled to Indianapolis Museum of Art; Tucson Museum of Art; Museum of Art, Carnegie Institute, Pittsburgh.*

Pennsylvania Academy of the Fine Arts, Philadelphia. *Contemporary American Realism Since 1960.* Traveled through 1983 to Virginia Museum of Fine Arts, Richmond; The Oakland Museum, Calif.

Herbert F. Johnson Museum, Cornell University, Ithaca, N.Y. *Art Faculty Exhibition.*

1982
Allan Frumkin Gallery, New York. *Contemporary Self-Portraits, Part 1: From the Mirror.**

Museum of Fine Arts, Boston. *A Private Vision: Contemporary Art from the Graham Gund Collection.**

Brainerd Art Gallery, State University of New York, Potsdam. *Contemporary Realism.* Traveled to Plaza Gallery, State University of New York, Albany.*

Laguna Beach Museum of Art, Calif. *The Real Thing: Southern California Realist Painting.**

1983
Allentown Art Museum, Pa. *The Artist's Studio in American Painting 1840-1983.**

Contemporary Arts Museum, Houston. *American Still Life 1945-1983.* Traveled through 1984 to Albright-Knox Art Gallery, Buffalo; Columbus Museum of Art, Ohio; Neuberger Museum, State University of New York, Purchase; Portland Art Museum, Oregon.

Pennsylvania Academy of the Fine Arts, Philadelphia. *Perspectives on Contemporary American Realism: Works of Art on Paper from the Collection of Jalane and Richard Davidson.* Traveled to The Art Institute of Chicago.*

University Art Museum, University of California, Santa Barbara. *Representational Drawing Today: A Heritage Renewed.* Traveled to Oklahoma Art Center, Oklahoma City; Elvehjem Museum of Art, University of Wisconsin, Madison; Colorado Springs Fine Arts Center.*

1984
International Exhibitions Foundation, Washington, D.C. *Twentieth-Century American Drawings: The Figure in Context.* Traveled through 1985 to Terra Museum of American Art, Evanston, Ill.; The Arkansas Arts Center, Little Rock; The Oklahoma Museum of Art, Oklahoma City; The Toledo Museum of Art, Ohio; Elvehjem Museum of Art, University of Wisconsin, Madison; The National Academy of Design, New York.*

The Maryland Institute, College of Art, Baltimore. *Drawings by Contemporary American Figurative Artists.*

1985
Isetan Museum, Tokyo. *American Realism: The Precise Image.* Traveled to the Daimaru Museum, Osaka; Yokohama Takashimana, Yokohama.*

San Francisco Museum of Modern Art. *American Realism: Twentieth-Century Drawings and Watercolors from the Glenn C. Janss Collection.* Travels through 1987 to De Cordova and Dana Museum and Park, Lincoln, Mass.; Archer M. Huntington Art Gallery, University of Texas, Austin; Mary and Leigh Block Gallery, Northwestern University, Evanston, Ill.; Williams College Museum of Art, Williamstown, Mass.; Akron Art Museum; Madison Art Center, Wis.*

*A catalogue or brochure accompanied the exhibition.

Selected Bibliography

Books and Catalogues

Akron Art Museum. *Selections in Contemporary Realism.* 1974.

Allentown, Pa., Allentown Art Museum. *The Artist's Studio in American Painting 1840-1983.* 1983.

Arthur, John. *Realist Drawings and Watercolors.* Boston: New York Graphic Society, 1980.

_____ . *Realists at Work.* New York: Watson-Guptill Publications, 1983.

Boston, Museum of Fine Arts. *A Private Vision: Contemporary Art from the Graham Gund Collection.* 1982. Essays by Carl Belz, Kathy Halbreich, Kenworth Moffett, Elisabeth Sussman, and Diane W. Upright.

Goodyear, Frank Jr. *Contemporary American Realism Since 1960.* Boston: New York Graphic Society, 1981.

Laguna Beach, Calif., Laguna Beach Museum of Art. *The Real Thing: Southern California Realist Painting.* 1982. Essay by Lynn Gamwell.

Lincoln, Mass., De Cordova and Dana Museum and Park. *The Super-Realist Vision.* 1973.

Los Angeles, Los Angeles Municipal Art Gallery. *Separate Realities: Developments in California Representational Painting and Sculpture.* 1973.

Lucie-Smith, Edward. *American Art Now.* New York: William Morrow and Company, Inc., 1985.

New York, Allan Frumkin Gallery. *The Big Still Life.* 1979.

_____ . *James Valerio: New Paintings and Drawings.* 1983.

Newport Beach, Calif., Newport Harbor Art Museum. *Inside/Out: Self Beyond Likeness.* 1981. Essays by Lynn Gamwell and Victoria Kogan.

Potsdam, Brainerd Art Gallery, State University of New York. *Contemporary Realism.* 1982. Essay by Joseph Hildreth.

San Antonio, San Antonio Museum of Art. *Real, Really Real, Super Real.* 1981. Interview by Sally Meredith-Boothe.

San Francisco, San Francisco Museum of Modern Art. *American Realism: Twentieth-Century Drawings and Watercolors from the Glenn C. Janss Collection.* 1985. Essay by Alvin Martin.

_____ . *Painting and Sculpture in California: The Modern Era.* 1977.

Santa Barbara, University Art Museum, University of California, Santa Barbara. *Representational Drawing Today: A Heritage Renewed.* 1983.

Tokyo, Isetan Museum. *American Realism: The Precise Image.* 1985. Essay by John Arthur.

Tulsa, Okla., Philbrook Art Center. *Realism/Photorealism.* 1980. Essay by John Arthur.

Washington, D.C., International Exhibitions Foundation. *Twentieth-Century American Drawings: The Figure in Context.* 1984. Essay by Paul Cummings.

Articles and Reviews

Apesos, Anthony. "Contemporary Realists Eschew Academic Norms." *New Art Examiner* 10 (Summer 1983): 10-11.

Arthur, John. "Interview with James Valerio." *American Artist* 47 (December 1983): 42-47, 97-99.

Artner, Alan. "Art: James Valerio." *Chicago Tribune* (November 13, 1981): 4/11.

_____ . "Valerio: Chicagoan's Art Hits Vein of Realism." *Chicago Tribune* (November 15, 1984): 5/7a.

Bell, Jane. "Reviews: James Valerio." *Arts Magazine* 48 (June 1974): 56.

Elliott, David. "A Young Realist Rising." *Chicago Sun-Times* (November 8, 1981): 5/23.

Frank, Peter. "Reviews: James Valerio." *Art News* 73 (October 1974): 123.

Kramer, Hilton. "Art: Narrative Painting Struggles for a Rebirth." *New York Times* (April 5, 1981): C18.

Schulman, Daniel. "Reviews: Contemporary Self-Portraits." *Arts Magazine* 57 (February 1983): 37.

Wolff, Theodore. "Narrative Art — Painting That Tells You a Story." *Christian Science Monitor* (April 13, 1981): 19.

James Valerio

23
Still Life #2 1978
Oil on canvas
93½ × 116 inches
Collection of
Mr. and Mrs. Graham Gund

24

Card Trick 1979
Oil on canvas
93½ × 116 inches
Collection of
The Alpert Family Trust

Checkers 1980
Oil on canvas
83⅝ × 96 inches
Collection of
The Alpert Family Trust

26

Still Life on Bedspread 1980
Oil on canvas
72 × 82 inches
Collection of The University of
Iowa Museum of Art, 1980.190

27

Self-Portrait 1981
Oil on canvas
92¼ × 75⅝ inches
Collection of
Mr. and Mrs. Joseph D. Shein

Pat Combing Her Hair 1983
Oil on canvas
92 × 100 inches
Courtesy Allan Frumkin Gallery,
New York and Struve Gallery,
Chicago

29

Night Fires 1984
Oil on canvas
92 × 100 inches
Collection of The Northern
Trust Company

Still Life with Tomatoes, 1985
Oil on canvas
78 × 105 inches
Courtesy Allan Frumkin Gallery,
New York

Acknowledgments

Many individuals participated in the organization of *Painting at Northwestern: Conger, Paschke, Valerio.* Elizabeth Shepherd, Block Gallery curator, organized innumerable details, and Deborah Thurston, department assistant, provided expert clerical support. James Riggs-Bonamici, Block Gallery registrar and preparator, coordinated the transportation arrangements as well as conceived and implemented the installation of the exhibition. The biographical and bibliographical material for the catalogue was compiled by Amy Mizrahi, Block Gallery graduate research assistant, aided by Denise Jennings and Cory Lund; they are due much credit. The editing of the text material was superbly handled by Nancy Liskar of Northwestern's Department of University Relations. Her thoroughness is evident throughout this catalogue. Hayward Blake, Rhonda Inouye, and Kay Fulton were responsible for the design and production of the catalogue; their creativity, meticulousness, and good humor are gratefully acknowledged. Paul Baker, Paul Baker Typography, and Rudy Rohner, Rohner Printing, are due special thanks for meeting seemingly impossible deadlines and for producing work of the highest quality.

Throughout this project, the Block Gallery has also benefited from the assistance and expertise of William Conger; Ed Paschke; James Valerio; Ann and Roy Boyd, Roy Boyd Gallery; Sonia Zaks, Zaks Gallery; William Bengtson, Phyllis Kind Gallery; Deborah and Bill Struve, Struve Gallery; George Adams, Allan Frumkin Gallery; Dennis Adrian; John Arthur; Mary Mathews Gedo; Michele Vishny; Richard Johnson, Northwestern University Language Laboratory; Gerrie Gartner, Department of Art Theory and Practice; Lee Yost, Department of University Relations; Peter Butterfield; Michael Tropea; Liane Thatcher, Graham Gund Collection; Bill Niffenegger, State of Illinois Center; Carole Peterson and Terry Suhre, Illinois State Museum; Mary Chiappetta, Marina Bank; Mary Todd, Needham Harper Worldwide; E. B. Smith, Jr., The Northern Trust Company; and JoAnn Conklin, The University of Iowa Museum of Art. To all those who have assisted, we offer our sincere appreciation.

KKF

Colophon

Typography: Optima Bold and Regular, Roman and Italic.

Paper: Centura Dull, Cover Basis 100. Centura Dull, Text Basis 100. Gainsborough, Text Basis 80, Charcoal End Sheets.

Printing: Offset Lithography.

Photography:
William H. Bengtson: Adrian Figure 3; Vishny Figures 1, 2, 4, 7, 8; and Color Plates 13-22.

eeva-inkeri: Adrian Figure 4.

Michael Tropea: Adrian Figures 1 and 2; Gedo Figures 1, 2, 4-7; Vishny Figure 3; and Color Plates 1-12, 28 and 29.

Tom van Eynde: Vishny Figure 5.

Design: Hayward Blake and Company.

Typography: Paul Baker Typography, Inc.

Printing: Rohner Printing Company.

Printed in the United States of America.